DETOUR

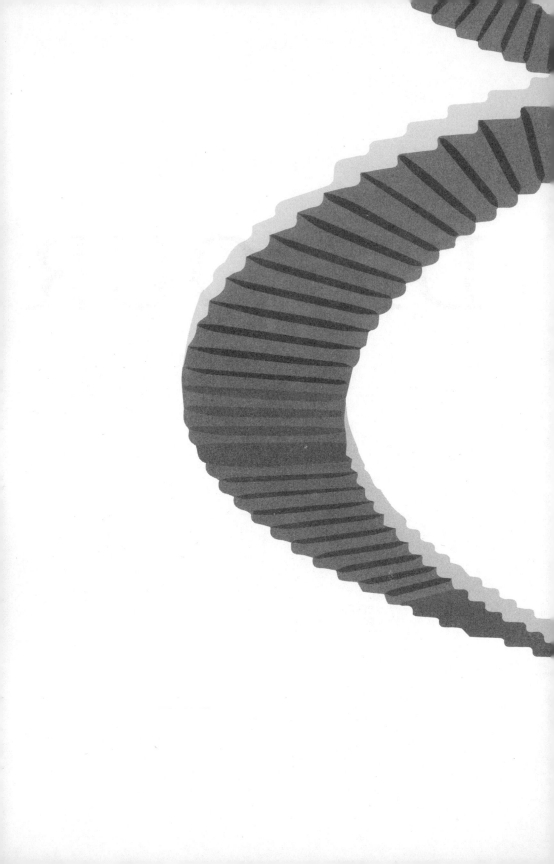

DETOUR

Developing the mindset to

NAVIGATE LIFE'S TURNS

STEVE GILLILAND

Published by Advantage, Charleston, South Carolina.
Member of Advantage Media Group.

ADVANTAGE is a registered trademark and the Advantage colophon is a trademark of Advantage Media Group, Inc.

Printed in the United States of America.

ISBN: 978-1-59932-540-8
LCCN: 2015938957

Book design by George Stevens.

This publication is designed to provide accurate and authoritative information in regard to the subject matter covered. It is sold with the understanding that the publisher is not engaged in rendering legal, accounting, or other professional services. If legal advice or other expert assistance is required, the services of a competent professional person should be sought.

Advantage Media Group is proud to be a part of the Tree Neutral® program. Tree Neutral offsets the number of trees consumed in the production and printing of this book by taking proactive steps such as planting trees in direct proportion to the number of trees used to print books. To learn more about Tree Neutral, please visit **www.treeneutral.com**. To learn more about Advantage's commitment to being a responsible steward of the environment, please visit **www.advantagefamily.com/green**

Advantage Media Group is a publisher of business, self-improvement, and professional development books and online learning. We help entrepreneurs, business leaders, and professionals share their Stories, Passion, and Knowledge to help others Learn & Grow. Do you have a manuscript or book idea that you would like us to consider for publishing? Please visit **advantagefamily.com** or call **1.866.775.1696.**

This book is dedicated to Diane,

who has always been way out of my league,

but has never left my side.

CONTACT STEVE

HALL OF FAME SPEAKER

**To schedule Steve to speak
at your event, call:**

866-445-5452

For more information, go to:

www.stevegilliland.com

ACKNOWLEDGMENTS

To
Every
Person
And
Circumstance
That
Crossed
My
Path
And
Took
Me
On
A
Roundabout
Route
Which
Allowed
Me
To
Change
And
Grow
Along
The
Way

IT'S THE

CURVES IN LIFE

[THAT MAKE US STRONG]

The 3 C's of Life

Choices – Chances – Changes

You must make a choice
to take a chance
or your life will never change.

CONTENTS

If it doesn't challenge you,
it doesn't change you.

INTRODUCTION

Imagine you are shot down over enemy territory, captured and kept in the dark for five and a half years as a prisoner of war. Visualize going that long without seeing a sunrise, sunset or the stars at night. What would you do if you were locked behind concrete walls and steel bars, yearning for your freedom? Whereas, you would experience long periods of reflection, your physical body wouldn't be the only part of your imprisonment. Your mind would be in repression and in constant danger of adopting an unhealthy outlook. While all of the accounts I have read regarding American POWs describe the horrors of confinement, most also address the resilient mindset necessarily developed to maintain a positive outlook in spite of circumstances.

In this lifetime, you will undoubtedly never experience the ordeal of being a POW, but chances are you will experience the suppression that simply comes with the human experience. We survive by coping, thriving and assuming a mindset that provides emotional balance. No one grows up in a perfect home with perfect parents, teachers, coaches, bosses and friends. Along the way, we all become disappointed, disillusioned or hurt in some way. The key is to gain strength from hardship and exploit it as a gift. Regrettably, though, even learning from our setbacks can trigger a downside by causing us to overcompensate.

I grew up in a lower middle class family, where we were conditioned to believe that working in a blue-collar job was an inevitable part of growing up in western Pennsylvania. You worked hard and made enough money to put a roof over your head and, with any luck, paid all your monthly bills. The majority of people I knew had this mindset and, much to my surprise, accepted it without issue. I was determined to escape from this thinking. I worked two jobs to put myself through college and worked even harder after I graduated. The downside is that I overcorrected to achieve this mindset and developed into a workaholic, severely impacting relationships with family, friends and my inner self.

We all make choices that force us to change direction. One day you're driving down a four-lane interstate with no traffic, the next you're on a two-lane road in bumper-to-bumper traffic during a blinding rainstorm. When you take wrong turns in life, you can't play the victim and relish in the role. You have to make a conscious effort to rewrite your story and steer yourself back on track, which takes discipline and courage. Laziness or miscalculation can have dire consequences on your home and work life.

In the previous decades in American culture, an emphasis was placed on character—our kindness, gentleness, serving spirit and concern for people here and around the world. These were non-negotiable for success in business and life. I feel we've changed. As the late Stephen Covey once stated, "We now place a greater emphasis on what we produce externally versus who we are internally. When the emphasis is put on what we can produce externally, we become people manipulators, motivated by goals and objectives set by others instead of those rooted in the values of our character."

To face the detours of life, get back to character and develop a mindset to live from the inside out. Be authentically successful by aligning your inner, private life and outer, public life with the same principles. Sadly, some of our nation's leaders and our most beloved professional athletes defend their inconsistent lifestyles by trying to convince us that what they do in their private lives should have no bearing on their performance at work or our perception of them. Don't buy into such hypocrisy! As you drive down the road and encounter unforeseen obstacles, turns and even dead ends, remain true to your core, and you'll be better equipped to navigate such challenges.

DETOUR will help you *Enjoy The Ride*™ wholly by learning how to navigate life's turns when something happens by chance and sets you on a course that you never planned, into a future you never imagined.

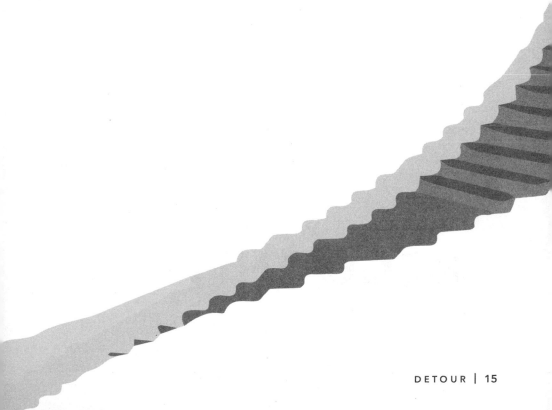

1

THE MINDSET OF
RECOGNITION

Identifying the Prerequisites for Change

rec·og·ni·tion

[re-kig-ˈni-shən]

noun

1. the action or process of recognizing or being recognized, in particular.

2. identification of a thing or person from previous encounters or knowledge.

3. acknowledgment of something's existence, validity, or legality.

Never Saw It Coming

"Year after year, decade after decade, we have seen problems papered over and tough choices kicked down the road, even as foreign competitors outpaced us. Well, we have reached the end of the road," said President Barack Obama in 2009, at a press conference announcing that the federal government was loaning $77 billion to GM and Chrysler. An amazing U-turn considering that, in 1955, GM became the first corporation in history to earn a billion dollars of revenue. Ironically, by the end of that decade, GM was so powerful that the Justice Department considered breaking it up like they would eventually do to the Bell System in 1982.

> No rational decisions can be made without taking into account the way things are and predicting what they will someday be.

What happened? The paramount problem was GM didn't see that a detour was coming up until it was too late. Instead of listening to customers and heeding the competition from afar, they never recognized a need to change. During the boom years of the auto industry, Detroit was the Silicon Valley of the golden age. At one point, it was the fourth most populous city in the country. As with the gold rush, everyone wanted a piece of the fortunes that were overflowing in a city that quickly became known for the highest median income in America. It became the first city to assign individual telephone numbers and pave a mile of concrete road. By July 2013, though, Detroit's population declined 26 percent from 1.85 million in 1950 to 706,000. The unemployment rate hit 18.6 percent, with per capita income at $15,261 a year. Detroit didn't burst overnight. Three and a half years prior to the federal bailout, GM lost $82 billion and the city of Detroit didn't have one produce-carrying grocery chain in the whole city. Once symbols of progress, both GM and Detroit became ill-fated casualties. GM and Detroit would teach us that no rational decisions can be made without taking into account the way things are and predicting what they will someday be. We would begin to put more analysis into understanding, anticipating and preparing for changes. While no one can really predict the future, we are now more apt to recognize what could happen and, in some cases, what should happen.

Too Much Apathy

When you think about Levi Strauss, Kodak, Zenith, Firestone, Timex, Nestle, U.S. Steel, Polaroid, Sears and IBM, what do these companies all have in common? They used to be the leaders in their respective industries. So how did they lose their market position? They all fashioned a culture that believed that nothing could slow them down; hence, they didn't see a need to change. In the 1960s, a man named Thomas Watson, Jr., who was the chief executive officer of IBM, moved the company's headquarters from the epicenter of Manhattan to an old apple orchard about thirty miles to the north. His reason was that he wanted his company to survive a nuclear attack on New York City. Nothing else seemed threatening to the gigantic corporation. IBM was so powerful and invincible that it seemed only a nuclear-powered missile could bring about its demise. Seventy percent of all money spent on computers went to IBM, and the remaining 30 percent was fought over by a bunch of rivals known as the "seven dwarfs." IBM made more money than any company in the world. It sold mainframe computers that were the size of refrigerators for $4 million apiece and kept $3 million for profit. While they made plenty of money in the other business segments, the mainframe piece made an easy $4 billion a year in profits.

> Whenever you are winning you always seem to be invincible.

While *Fortune* magazine was calling Watson "the greatest capitalist in history," and executives worldwide named IBM the company they most admired, some at IBM began predicting that the big, costly computers would be replaced by networks of smaller, cheaper computers and that the company had to change. Regrettably, no one was listening. Moreover, IBM substantiated the truism that whenever you are winning you always seem to be invincible. Fearing the company's vulnerability, some of the most talented and thoughtful individuals abandoned ship. When IBM offered early retirement, the smartest people took the chance to get out. In 1990, the company began the new decade by turning a profit of $6 billion for the year. Then, suddenly, IBM began to collapse. The competition was selling workstations that cost less than $100,000 and fit on top of a desk. It didn't make sense to customers to pay $4 million dollars for IBM's enormous mainframes. Over the next two years, IBM cut prices by 50 percent, then by 70 percent. It didn't matter. In 1992, IBM lost the largest sum of money that any corporation had ever lost in a single year. The $5-billion-dollar loss plummeted their stock price from $43 to $12 a share, with shareholders losing a total of $75 billion. There wasn't enough cash to cover payroll, and the lifetime employment promise ended with a mass layoff of 140,000 workers. When the dust had settled, the company that was once unshakable recognized that they could either change or vanish. The biggest challenge would be shifting their approach. When you're locked into a mindset that helps you succeed, it's difficult even to think about the profound changes you'll have to respond to.

Answers Without Questions

They say you don't know what you have until it's gone. The truth is, you know exactly what you have; you just never believe you'll lose it. You think everything's fine, that nothing needs to change—until it's too late. You disregard anyone else's feelings as well as your own need to change and grow, because those conflict with your desire to maintain the status quo.

> It's easier to focus attention on what you don't want instead of taking control of what's in front of you.

You're passive. You wait for something to happen, then evaluate whether it was positive or negative and respond accordingly. While you express a desire to map out a successful future, you continue to be reactive instead of proactive. It's easier to focus attention on what you don't want instead of taking control of what's in front of you—your family, your job, your mental and physical well-being, your other blessings. Positive change will not happen until you recognize what you have power over.

Adjusting Without Changing

People have an instinctive ability to adapt to most situations and often live by the adage, "It is what it is." Regrettably, while our ability to adapt is amazing, our ability to change isn't. When you least expect it, life challenges your courage and willingness to change. In such moments, you can either accept it for what it is or make it what you want. Just as failure is an inevitable, vital part of success, every detour is a critical part of your trip. Detours allow you to exercise creativity and resourcefulness by moving forward in ways you had not anticipated.

> When you least expect it,
> life challenges your courage
> and willingness to change.
> In such moments, you can
> either accept it for what it is
> or make it what you want.

Two weeks before my 45th birthday, while sitting in my mother's living room, I revealed that, after just one year and ten months of marriage, my wife had demanded a divorce—my second such failure. Mom's response astonished me. As I spoke, she sat silently, tears forming in her eyes, staring at me with a look of unease and compassion that only a mother can express without saying a word. When I finished articulating my side of the story— which, admittedly, was not entirely objective—she said calmly but with unnerving resolve, "Son, you need to recognize that you have to change. You're the only common denominator in both marriages." Mom's words were a huge wake-up call. I realized that while I had been adjusting my life to accommodate the changes that marriage brought into it, I wasn't doing more. I stopped growing, as if that were the end of my road and nothing further was needed from me. A detour—such as divorce—is what you make it. It can be the beginning of something new and beautiful, or it can stop you dead. When you look within and diagnose your own need to change—for yourself as well as for those to whom you're committed—you will grow.

Writing Your Own Story

Each of us has a unique story, a distinct life. When we're dissatisfied with ourselves, we sometimes covet the lives of those around us. But are those objects of our envy truly experiencing the lives they want? Unless you know them as well as you know yourself, you can't answer that question. They may be living a life they *think* they want or that they've convinced themselves is the best they can hope for. Sometimes it's easier to pretend to be what we aren't than to become who we should be.

> If you're searching for someone who can change your life, well, look in the mirror.

Consider the difference between a costume and a uniform. A costume is something you wear pretending to be something else. A uniform, however, is a reflection of who you are within. Sometimes we spend a lifetime trying on different costumes while searching for that one person or one career we believe will fit us just right. If you're searching for someone who can change your life, well, look in the mirror. You and you alone are the key. Don't rely on external validation to feel good about yourself. Start building stability within and an inner spring that energizes you with positivity no matter what others say or do. You weren't born to fit in; you were born to stand out.

Carving Out a New Normal

To navigate life's turns, recognize your strengths, trust the true nature of who you are and commit. If others don't understand you, that's their hurdle, not yours. What matters most is that you understand yourself. This is not your practice life—this is your *actual* life.

> If others don't understand you, that's their hurdle, not yours.

It's time for you to carve out a new, more authentic normal for yourself. Figure out who you really are and what you really want. Don't settle—settling leads to frustration and misery, jealousy and pain. Be comfortable with being uncomfortable. Change your mindset. Steer clear of complacency and lazy thinking unless you're willing to accept complete responsibility for the disappointing results. When you take ownership of your life, you control your happiness and self-esteem. Is it scary to push yourself? Is it difficult? You bet. Just remember that every loss, setback or hurdle can either be a dead end or an opportunity to grow. The choice is yours. Every detour you face in life becomes exactly what you make it.

Choose Wisely

There are many reasons why change is good for you. For me, the single most important reason is that change is opportunity. Without change, things stay the same and ultimately will deteriorate and perish. One literal example is healthcare. Despite spending $2.1 trillion a year in the U.S. alone, it appears that we are not feeling any healthier. The reason—our choices! So many of us are sick because of how we choose to live our lives, not because of factors beyond our control. Articles in several periodicals support that 80 percent of the healthcare budget is consumed by five behavioral issues. Smoking, drinking and eating are the top three, followed closely by lack of exercise and too much stress.

> Change is possible even in situations that seem hopeless.

In 2003, I had a heart attack. My cardiologist put it bluntly. He said, "If you want to stop the course of your heart disease before it kills you, then you have to switch to a healthier lifestyle. You have to drink judiciously, stop overeating, start exercising and relieve your stress." Yet, even with the knowledge I have a very bad disease and know I should change, I struggle. Sadly, I am not alone. While we would like to think that facts could convince people to change, and we believe people are essentially rational, the truth is that most people don't change even when the right choice can improve their lives. Knowledge may be power, and the truth may set you free, but for many people it just doesn't make a difference. The good news is that change is possible even in situations that seem hopeless. Whether you are struggling with a stressful life or have come up against an unexpected challenge, you can change the deep-rooted patterns of how you think, feel and act.

Everything Happens for a Reason

My inner circle of family and friends would collectively agree that, while I have always been rather successful in achieving my professional goals, I grappled to find stability in my personal life. Instead of doing what I knew I should do, too many times I did what I wanted to do and then made excuses to justify my actions. Regardless of how illogical it was, the discipline that defined my success eluded my private life. The problem was I didn't see the problem because I was the biggest part of the problem. For every relationship that failed there was an explanation that permitted me to deny any change was necessary. Even more absurd was that, even though I knew I needed to fix the situation, I refused to because of my fear of failing and feeling vulnerable. I was convinced I could never change because I would never trust again.

> People don't change,
> their priorities do.

Sometimes people come into your life and you know right away that they were meant to be there, to serve a purpose like helping you figure out who you are and who you need to become. For me, it was a complete stranger on an airplane who would impact my life in a profound way. At 37,000 feet, an elderly man sitting beside me for a two-hour flight would talk to me like we were lifelong friends. I can still remember him saying, "Everything happens for a reason." As I shared my marital and dating misfortunes, he listened like an expert therapist. "Sometimes things happen that can't be explained and seem unfair, but they also can serve as lessons to help us realize our potential," he said. He talked about people early in his life who hurt and betrayed him. I recall him talking about how the older he got the more he appreciated every moment, and that one of the greatest eye-openers for him was when he learned that people don't change, their priorities do. A lot of our conversation focused on my priorities, which all centered on my career as an author and speaker. The more I talked to this total stranger, the more I realized how many walls I had put around my heart. While I was guaranteed to never get hurt again, I was also missing out on all of the amazing things that a relationship brings. In 120 minutes, he helped me recognize that once I was able to overcome the pain I would be one step closer to finding the one that lasts forever. Of course, this doesn't mean we can ever know for certain that someone won't hurt us again. The only way we can know if we're able to trust someone is by first giving them trust. That means being vulnerable and recognizing that where we have been and what we have experienced will sanction us to circumnavigate the diversions along the way.

Develop Discipline

When you are consistent in doing the things you know you should do, when you know you should do them, you will enjoy a more rewarding and satisfying life. The late personal development legend Jim Rohn said, "We must all suffer one of two things: the pain of discipline or the pain of regret." Being disciplined gives you the strength to withstand the detours and difficulties, whether physical, emotional or mental. Every time you push yourself to do something you know you should do, you are building your self-esteem. Self-esteem is a result of self-discipline that involves acting according to what you think instead of how you feel in the moment. Often, it involves sacrificing the pleasure and thrill of the moment for what matters most in life.

> Discipline is one of the cornerstones to living a successful and fulfilling life.

Discipline is freedom. You may not agree with this statement, and if you do there are certainly others who would share your opinion. For many people, discipline is associated with the absence of freedom. In fact, the opposite is true. As the late Stephen Covey once wrote, "The undisciplined are slaves to moods, appetites and passions." Undisciplined people lack the freedom that comes with possessing particular skills and abilities like playing a musical instrument or speaking a foreign language. Discipline is one of the cornerstones to living a successful and fulfilling life and something we should all strive to master. As you move down the highway of life, curves in the road, blind spots and unexpected detours will all require discipline.

Accept the Positive Results

If you regularly describe your current job as boring, mundane or menial, chances are you have come to a detour in your career. One of the most positive aspects of change is that it is never boring. On the contrary, it can create a new excitement and energy that gives us the spark we need to keep moving in the right direction. It fuels a passion that is only experienced when we are challenged to learn new things, meet new people, grow as professionals and take risks that push us to reach our potential. None of that can happen unless we are willing to experience the fear that inevitably arises when we move out of our comfort zones.

> If fear, pain and hard work are prerequisites of change, it is easy to understand why some people resist it.

Sometimes the roadblocks we encounter force us to make decisions that can ultimately reshape our entire lives. When people ask me how a resident of western Pennsylvania for 46 years ended up in North Carolina, I respond by letting them know that

I wanted passion back in my life. I had to be willing to meet the challenge of change regardless of the fear, risk and trepidation of moving away from my family. For some people, it involves going back to school, taking on new responsibilities or redefining a career path. For me, it meant starting a new life with a woman who would create a better future for my family and me. I would be required to step outside my comfort zone and not be content with playing it safe. It also allowed me to see why, if fear, pain and hard work are prerequisites of change, it is easy to understand why some people resist it. When I ask people why they won't risk improving their current situation, they provide the best-sounding reasons why changing isn't right for them. Just like GM, Detroit and IBM, you have to modify your attitude and behavior before it's too late. Think about what you really want. If you are open to new things, see a detour as a new opportunity and welcome the change, you will always be growing. Remember, no risk, no fear; no fear, no passion—and no growth.

Bad Days Teach Good Lessons

It's hard some days to stay positive, especially when having a bad day. It's hard to stay positive when things are tough financially, emotionally or physically. However, in order to change, we must be willing to look at these challenges in a positive manner. In essence, we must be willing to reevaluate situations with an unbiased mindset. The more detours we face, the easier it is to become pessimistic and overlook the lessons that failures and losses can teach us. The danger is that negativity relieves the temporary feelings and emotions one feels; however, over time, it affects the actions and rationality of a person. It produces a byproduct of negativity, which is worrying. Worry often comes through constant reevaluation of poor choices or the feeling we are not in control of a situation. It is human nature to obsess about all that could go wrong, but forgetting about the things you can't control empowers you to concentrate on what you can. When something goes wrong, we tend to compound the situation by focusing on the negative instead of finding solutions. The only way to turn a bad day into a good day is through awareness. We tend not to change what we are not aware of.

> Experience is not what happens to you, it is what you do with what happens to you.

I consistently encourage others by emphasizing that with every new day comes new opportunity, and new opportunity is the catalyst for change. Experiencing bad days allows us to see what we need to do, so that we don't repeat our previous blunders. The more we are willing to diminish the bad days and change the negative aspects of our lives, the less difficult it becomes to adapt to change. We all face issues that can upset our day, but perspective determines whether or not those issues become bigger than they should. By perspective, I mean that interpreting situations that occur in everyday life is the key to solving our worries and changing our mindset. Complaining about a terrible day is tempting, but stressing out won't make you feel any better. If you search for the lesson in your present struggle, you'll be able to make positive changes that would prevent similar situations in the future. Experience is not what happens to you, it is what you do with what happens to you. You embody every experience you have had in your life every single day—even the bad ones. Let every experience become a lesson that shapes your mindset.

You Are Not a Victim

As long as we think that someone or something else is responsible for our problems, our situation is hopeless. Not owning up to our actions takes away our part in doing anything differently. We simply remain stuck while continuing to complain and feel miserable. We ultimately become what we believe ourselves to be. If you tell yourself you can't do something, you never will. If you believe in yourself despite struggles and frustrations, however, you will have a much better chance. Retain your power by not blaming others.

> You don't need to join every argument you are invited to.

Assigning blame and making excuses keeps you victimized. You don't have to do anything different because it's not about you, it's about someone or something else. You're simply the recipient. While you are, in fact, the recipient of external forces outside your control, you have control over your reactions and responses. Looking at yourself and your responses may require you to do something different or try something new. That can be frightening. You can move forward. Be selective in your battles. Have the mindset to be happy, not right. You don't need to join every argument you are invited to. Even the darkest night will eventually end, and the sun will rise. If you take another step, and another, you'll be surprised how far you can go beyond what you thought was the endpoint.

Acknowledge You Need Help

At some point, we come to realize that even when we think a situation is hopeless, there's usually a different way, a way out. The reason we can't see it is because it's outside our intangible structure or we have given up because we're discouraged by past disappointments. The situation that seems impossible to us, with our mindsets and skill sets, sometimes can be solved if we simply recognize our need for help. In my book *Enjoy The Ride*, I remind people to not take things personally because life picks on everyone. Living the good life involves some amount of necessary pain. You will make mistakes and encounter heartbreaking detours during the journey. The only way to grow is to learn from them, and the only way to learn from them is to sometimes ask for direction.

> Letting go of what
> isn't working makes
> way for what will.

When everything you try fails, when things aren't adding up in your life and when you have no place to turn, there is no shame in starting over by changing things up. It's tough letting go of the old and conceding that some circumstances may be hopeless. Letting go of what isn't working makes way for what will. On the other hand, occasionally stepping away from a situation can help you obtain a different viewpoint. The Stone Age didn't end because they ran out of stones. It ended because people began to identify and recognize the benefits of working with metals, such as the ability to more easily form tools. Undoubtedly, working with bronze, an alloy of copper and tin, for the first time would have been defined as a "thinking outside the box" moment for early man. The Stone Age ended because there were better and more efficient technologies—and humankind recognized their need to change.

The Rest of the Story

It's been said that there's a fine line between genius and insanity. Some of the most famous outliers include Albert Einstein, whose teachers thought he would never amount to much. Walt Disney was fired for lacking imagination and not being creative enough. Decca Records rejected the Beatles because they didn't like their sound and thought they had no future in show business. In each case, these outliers faced enormous detours. They were dismissed by people inside their respective industries in positions of authority who had the ability to pass judgment.

As you read in this chapter, by 1993, IBM was in the midst of a near-death experience when its Board decided to dismiss its then born-and-bred IBM CEO and Chairman, John Akers, replacing him with outlier Lou Gerstner, who was President of Nabisco at the time. When IBM first made the announcement, Wall Street howled, "What did a man who made Oreo Cookies know about computers?" The response was, "Absolutely nothing." This was the genius of the Board's decision. Gerstner knew nothing of IBM's nostalgia, business strategy or corporate culture. He wasn't locked into the mindset that helped IBM to succeed. He had no friends at IBM and, thus, no mixed loyalties. He didn't have to worry about preserving ties to the company legacy. He was able to objectively evaluate and pass judgment on the entirety of the IBM organization and fashion a path to the future unhindered by IBM's past and its traditions.

As such, he transformed IBM from a company whose main business was selling computer hardware into a business services provider. By 2004, its annual profits rebounded to more than $8 billion, and its stock prices revived from $12 per share to $80 and higher. He was the perfect man, in the perfect situation, with the perfect mindset. As he approached this colossal DETOUR, he recognized what needed to be changed and executed it perfectly.

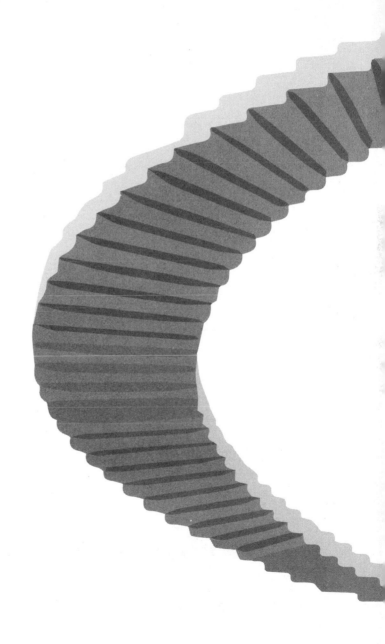

2

THE MINDSET OF
REACTION

Managing the Stress When Change Occurs

re·ac·tion

rē-ˈak-shən

noun

1. an action performed or a feeling experienced in response to a situation or event.

2. a person's ability to respond physically and mentally to external stimuli.

Unavoidable, But Manageable

Unless, by some miracle, you're lucky enough to be completely free of anger, worry, deadlines and any other source of tension in everyday life, you're going to feel a little stress now and then. Simply put, stress is our emotional and physiological response to anxiety-producing events, such as life's detours. Not only can this be profoundly unpleasant, it can seriously affect our health and work. We experience stress if we believe we don't have time, resources or knowledge to handle a situation. In short, when we feel out of control.

Understanding life's trials enables some of us to cope better than others. The good news is that you can manage stress so that it doesn't negatively affect you. So often, what brings us to our knees is not life itself, but our interpretation of life's challenges. Unloading certain demands, pressures and toxic people is a good foundation. Better nutrition, sleep and exercise—and surrounding yourself with upstanding people—are also beneficial.

> What brings us to our knees is not life itself, but our interpretation of life's challenges.

Whether triggered by confronting a wild tiger in the heart of the jungle or by encountering office politics in the corporate jungle, stress is a fact of life. It is unavoidable, but manageable.

Mastering it means developing the proper mindset to respond to change. Unlike in a tiger encounter, the stresses we face today—in our ever-changing, ultra-technological world—seem to be more pervasive but less tangible than at any other time. Consequently, our options for relief aren't as clear-cut. Society often prefers to medicate symptoms rather than alleviate the cause. The latter takes more work and self-analysis, of course, but it's more effective in the long term.

The negative impact of stress on the body is well-known: an elevated heart rate, high blood pressure, rapid breathing, gastro-intestinal discomfort and an increased risk of heart disease. Sleep disturbances, depression and stress may even contribute to degenerative diseases. Less well-known are the effects on brain function. A Canadian study in 2005 showed that increased stress hormones lead to memory impairment in the elderly and learning difficulties in young adults.

Burnout or Pressure

Juggling multiple projects and running on four hours of sleep is business as usual for some happy, healthy and successful people, while such a lifestyle pushes others over the brink. Some brag about how much pressure they are under, how they feast on it. The implication is that they are important and have been entrusted with a significant amount of responsibility. Some corporate cultures even create an atmosphere of continual pressure in an attempt to make their employees productive. Those who thrive are seen by colleagues as workaholics. Psychologists refer to them as resilient, or hardy, and say they share certain backgrounds and qualities that enable them to thrive. People who are highly resilient appreciate ongoing changes and enormous pressure. Others, however, face constant stress because they're maladaptive perfectionists who struggle to let go of tasks.

> Stress impacts our ability to do our jobs effectively, influences how we work with others and compromises our health.

As an acknowledged perfectionist, I have always struggled with change. I firmly believe that my fear of failure created a massive amount of stress. Nonetheless, my resilient nature has allowed me to flourish under pressure. It took a heart attack, though, to rattle my cage. I reevaluated my priorities both at home and work, deciding what was important and making some difficult choices.

I set limits. I realized I couldn't do EVERYthing—and neither could my wife. We sat down and set realistic expectations for finances, professional growth and personal wants. I simplified my life and focused on what I could control. One of the hardest things was learning to say "no" when a request or demand conflicted with my priorities or exceeded my limits—or challenged my innate need to prove I could do it all. I stopped giving in to guilt, stopped worrying that I might be letting people down even if it hurt me.

The results were amazing. For one, I became a more flexible and cooperative husband (I hope!). Instead of being irritable and getting angry at every little thing that wasn't complete—or completed the way I wanted—I was able to let go. I realized that much of what I'd been convincing myself for so long was vitally important was actually not at all.

The lessons are tough: stress impacts our ability to do our jobs effectively, influences how we interact with others and compromises our health. This can have a serious impact on our careers, relationships and well-being. So…when faced with a detour, be mindful of how you react. Evaluating any physical or emotional challenge with a more objective mindset than you're used to can serve you well in navigating life's turns. Be prepared.

Signs of Stress

It's important to learn how to recognize when your stress levels are out of control. The most dangerous thing about stress is how easily it can sneak up on you. You get so used to it that is starts to feel familiar and you often don't notice how much it's affecting you. It can take a heavy toll. Everyone reacts to stress differently, however. Some common signs and symptoms include:

- Frequent headaches
- Cold or sweaty hands and feet
- Frequent heartburn, stomach pain or nausea
- Panic attacks

- Excessive sleeping or insomnia

- Persistent concentration difficulties

- Obsessive or compulsive behaviors

- Social withdrawal or isolation

- Constant fatigue

- Irritability and angry episodes

- Significant weight gain or loss

- Continually feeling overwhelmed or overloaded

Because of the widespread damage stress can cause, it's important to know your own limit. Just how much stress is too much varies from person to person. Some of my friends, neighbors and family are able to roll with the punches, while many seem to collapse under and any amount of pressure. Then there's me. I thrive on the excitement and challenge of a high-stress lifestyle. Your own ability to tolerate stress depends on many factors, including the quality of your relationships, your general outlook, your emotional intelligence and genetics.

Remember the Big Picture

When we confront a situation, we make two subconscious judgments: first, whether it threatens our social standing, values, time, reputation or survival; second, whether we have the resources to meet it. The difference between those who are successful and those who aren't is not whether we suffer from stress—because we all do—but how we handle it. Keep things in perspective. As you'll read later in this book, there are three sides to every story. For now, a great example of big picture thinking is equating the immediate strains of exercise with the long-term benefits of getting healthier. For me, waking an hour earlier in the morning to open a book or journal isn't so much about finding time to read as it is about expanding my knowledge and, thus, helping my career.

> If you're too caught up in the details, nothing is ever going to change.

Just like a film with swooping panoramas and detailed close-ups, every aspect of your life involves several different focal lengths. Even as I am writing this book, I'm focused on this chapter; however, I take time to step back and look at the entire project periodically to remind myself of the big picture. It's too easy to veer off course. Details are certainly important, but it's easy to get bogged down in a mass of actions. If your life feels like a constant treadmill—running and running and never really getting anywhere—then you might find it difficult to maintain perspective. Unfortunately, if you're too caught up in the details, nothing is ever going to change. The daily grind and routine will never cease, and although you clear out your inbox and work twelve-hour days, every week is going to be the same. Take a mental break. Step back. Make some changes. Maybe that means taking a break from social media, bowing out of a monthly get-together with neighbors or avoiding, at least temporarily, anything else that might prevent you from putting some stressors to rest.

Chill Out

The *Hotel Chillout Resort* is situated at Jyatha just north from where Thamel, the only tourist center of Kathmandu, begins. The resort promotes itself as the perfect place to unwind and enjoy the very best it has to offer. It boasts a comfortable, happy and friendly environment. If only life provided the obsessive among us with a place where the glass was always half full and every lemon became lemonade—the same place where the balance between optimism and realism provides an environment of mental harmony. Thanks to the work ethic my mother instilled in me early on, I have always been able to carve out a simple way of living. Nonetheless, I also inherited her perfectionism, tension and regretfully bad temper. By nature, I am not a chilled-out person, but time and the assistance of my wife, children and six kitties have rehabilitated me. I have learned to react to things differently.

> You will never arrive at a place where everything is perfect and there are no worries.

As I have stated on hundreds of occasions, in front of thousands of people, there is no destination. It will always outdistance you. When you get one thing paid off, another will surface. When you get your children through middle school, there will be high school. When you make it through Friday, the next week will offer new challenges. You will never arrive at a place where everything is perfect and there are no worries. Life is about the big stuff, the little stuff and everything in between. I have found that to be "chilled out" you have to be organized to avoid the stress of uncertainty and indecision. When you know where you're going, how you're getting there and who is driving, you can relax. I have also learned that just because I know where I'm heading and have a plan to get there doesn't mean there won't be detours along the way. I might even have an accident, but my expectations are that the journey is not going to be perfect. Wait a minute, Mr. Positive Speaker! Did you just say don't strive for perfection? No, what I said was be optimistic with realistic expectations. When you finally can reach a point in life where you know and understand your strengths and weaknesses, you can improve what needs attention and accept your unshakable faults. You deserve the opportunity to check into your own Chillout Hotel and begin reducing stress by reacting differently to it.

Stop Pedaling the Stress Cycle

Occasionally, it may feel like we no sooner end one stressful situation and another appears without warning. We automatically evaluate the situation and determine the level of problem it may be to us. If we decide that the demands outweigh our skills and resources to meet the challenge, our nerves are rattled. Everyone sees and handles situations differently. There is no single right way of coping. Hey, whatever works—as long as we stop pedaling the stress cycle.

> Working hard for something
> we don't care about is
> called stress. Working
> hard for something we
> love is called passion.

Before you can do that you must determine whether you're analysis-oriented, emotion-oriented or distraction-oriented. For some people, analyzing a situation and taking immediate action is their coping mechanism. Emotional people tend to deal with their feelings and seek out social support. Others avoid a situation by distracting themselves with activities or work. Any one of these can reduce stress, but none will reduce the stressors. Learning to manage your time and make healthy choices both in your work and leisure time will.

For me, the best way to stop my stress cycle is by setting limits and giving myself permission to say "no." More times than I can remember, I would agree to attend a community event, charitable outing, neighborhood gathering or certain activities that didn't even interest me. I soon learned that working hard for something we don't care about is called *stress*. Working hard for something we love is called *passion*. I set unrealistic expectations and took on way too many projects. It was all more stressful than work. To all my family, friends and neighbors—sorry! When I kept realistic expectations, set limits and prioritized things as "Must vs. Can't wait," I felt a lot better. Ask yourself, are you wasting 100% of your energy on a 5% priority issue?

Adopt Manageable Routines

One of the paramount issues that we all face is how to respond to numerous interruptions. Today, just handling email can be overwhelming. The more I anticipate and plan for stressful situations, the better I cope with them. Facing an overload of email won't drain you if you're healthy enough to cope with that kind of anxiety. Alcohol, caffeine, sugar, fats and tobacco all strain your body's capacity to manage pressure. A diet with fruits, vegetables and whole grain foods will create the necessary energy to manage certain stressors. Slowing down and relaxing contributes to how well you respond to circumstances, too. Do you exercise? When is the last time you had a soothing massage? How about a vacation that's more about scenery than adventure? While it's important to play, there's a lot to be said for shutting down and appreciating the view.

> Friendships should be nourishing and not leave you feeling drained.

Then, there are those relationships. Friendships, social circles and support groups—all of these can be either rewarding or draining. Ever been in a social setting and ask yourself what you enjoy most about belonging? I will forever consider what my wife shared with me about a monthly gathering she used to attend. She described it as cliquish, with some of the women being aloof towards the whole assembly. When my wife decided to stop participating, a "friend" of hers said, "I may not like these women, but I'm still going to go. I may need one of them someday." Alrighty then! I'd call that senseless stress. Friendships should be nourishing, not draining. They should align with your sense of purpose, direction—and fun!

Constant Opportunity to Evolve

Change is inevitable, growth is optional. Likewise, growth means change. I also believe that stress is optional. We tend to perceive change as something adverse instead of positive because it forces us out of our comfort zone. Successful companies use change to their advantage, seeing it as an opportunity to develop. When you adopt that mindset, you make yourself "change-ready." Change-readiness is the ability to continually respond to detours in ways that create advantage, minimize risk and sustain performance.

> Change is the norm, and our level of stress is determined by our reaction to the situation and each other.

Just as companies must be prepared for change, we as individuals must constantly reinvent ourselves. Already with two sons from my first marriage, I became a stepfather in 2005. Early on, my responses to events related to my new stepsons were stressful, combative and, admittedly, incorrect at least 80% of the time. So, I challenged myself to evolve as a parent and develop childrearing skills that I lacked when raising my first two sons. I had always spent time with them, but confess that I didn't ask often enough, "What would you like to do?"

My biggest progression as a parent was when my stepsons, Adam and Alex, taught me to be open-minded. Naturally, they disagreed with me more than I liked, but I learned to allow them to express their opinions. It didn't take long for me to realize that controlling my stress level as a stepfather meant reacting more tolerantly to situations that went against what I had always considered good parental guidance. Adam and Alex taught me patience, which also permitted them to learn some valuable life lessons through the mistakes they made. As one of their role models, I stopped overreacting and showed them how to take responsibility, behave, work hard and achieve goals. Yes, we have encountered many detours and roadblocks in our relationship, but the stress level went down once all three of us recognized that change was the norm. It's been a parenting lesson that taught me "They will do as I do, not as I say."

Check Your Expectations

Are your expectation levels based on what you want to happen or what is likely to happen? Do those expectations take into consideration what others want or how they will be affected, or are they entirely self-centered? One big reason we sometimes overreact and become stressed out is because we fail to envision different outcomes or fully appreciate another point of view. I confess that I used to overreact to every little thing, and my feelings would utterly determine my state of mind. I took too much personally and made too many things a big deal—even positive experiences.

Overreactions allow you and others to push buttons that unhinge your ability to think calmly, to judge rationally. Just as I wrote in my book *Hide Your Goat*, it's important to understand what your triggers are. Those closest to you know them. Although they may not intentionally try to get on your last nerve, chances are, when they do, it isn't as much about them as it is about you.

> An overreaction is disproportionate to the problem at hand.

The best defense from overplaying a situation is to balance your expectations with perspective. If your spouse brings up your personal finances, don't automatically think you're being accused of mismanaging your money. He or she might simply be confessing that they're worried not just for you, but for both of you. We don't always express our concerns in the most eloquent manner, so step back and think about whether or not that person would really, honestly try to hurt or anger you. An overreaction is disproportionate to the problem at hand. You are far more likely to escalate a conflict when you exaggerate your response. Ask yourself, "Is this worth giving up my self-control?" Most detours won't drastically change your life and really don't impact your purpose and intentions. A month after a circumstance triggers your stress you oftentimes can't even remember why it bothered you so much. Missteps and poor choices happen. Keep high expectations for yourself and other people, yes, but don't allow single moments to overshadow your entire life experience. Perception is everything. A rollercoaster ride is terrifying for some but a thrill for others.

You Are Not to Blame

Stress is an unavoidable consequence of being human. If you can't avoid a situation, alter it. What steps can you take to prevent the problem from ever occurring again? Often this involves subtle changes in the way you operate in your daily life. If your child has a messy room, keep the door closed. If you can't avoid or alter a situation, accept it—and try not to place blame. This does not mean giving up; rather, it's changing the way you think. Recalibrate the circumstance from a more positive perspective. Single-parenting has its own brand of added pressures and levels of difficulty. You don't have a partner to balance the load and the decision-making. When an issue surfaces, ask yourself if you'd rather be a single parent or still be trapped in an emotionally abusive relationship for the sake of being married?

> When a situation is getting you down, focus on the positive.

My parents divorced early in their marriage. They were miserable together, had little respect for one another and tried to raise my brother and me in a home filled with anger, tension, arguments and discord. I can still remember my older brother begging them to stay together "like all of the other kids' parents." Today, looking back, I feel that one of the most fortunate things that happened to me as a child was that divorce. It's not that my parents were bad people; they were just totally mismatched. They couldn't communicate, and every argument was centered on winning at all costs.

Last year, my mother and stepfather celebrated their 50th wedding anniversary. That experience prompted me to reflect on my own divorce years ago, one in which children were involved. The split was unavoidable, and I refused to lay blame or let this major detour control me. Most gratifying now is to see my adult sons thriving emotionally and psychologically. They are happy, cooperative and respectful in their relationships. I am happily remarried myself. When a situation is getting you down, focus on the positive. Take a moment to reflect on all that you appreciate in your life, including your own unique qualities—and stop blaming yourself.

Tips to Manage Stress

Take a time-out. Stepping back from the problem helps clear your head.

Eat well-balanced meals. Do not skip meals. Be healthy.

Limit alcohol and caffeine. These can trigger anxiety and panic attacks.

Get enough sleep. Your body needs sufficient rest.

Exercise daily. You'll feel good and maintain better health.

Take deep breaths. Inhale and exhale slowly.

Count to 10 slowly. Repeat, and count to 100 if necessary.

Do your best. Instead of aiming for perfection, which
is impossible, be proud of your best effort.

Accept that you cannot control everything.

Put your stress in perspective.

Welcome humor. A good laugh goes a long way.

Maintain a positive attitude. Replace negative thoughts with upbeat ones.

Get involved. Volunteer or find another way to be active in your community.
This will create a support network and give you a break from everyday stress.

Learn what triggers your anxiety. Is it work, family,
school or something else you can identify?

Talk to someone. Tell friends and family you're feeling
overwhelmed, and let them know how they can help you. Talk
to a physician or therapist for a professional opinion.

3

THE MINDSET OF
REALITY

Discovering the Three Sides to the Story

re·al·i·ty

rē-ˈa-lə-tē

noun

1. the world or the state of things as
    they actually exist, as opposed to an
    idealistic or notional idea of them.

2. the state or quality of having
    existence or substance.

Mirrors Never Lie

In Disney's 1937 film *Snow White and the Seven Dwarfs*, the evil stepmother posed the question, "Mirror, mirror, on the wall, who in this realm is the fairest of them all?" The mirror would regularly answer, "You, my queen, are the most fair of all." With this reply, the stepmother was happy because she knew the mirror never lied.

> Reality is the difference between what we wish and what is.

Then one day, when Snow White was seven years old, the mirror had to fess up: "You, my queen, may have a beauty quite rare, but Snow White is a thousand times more fair." At that moment, the stepmother received a painful reality check—that is, the difference between what she wished and what was. Some would argue that what we wish for is defined as optimism and that without it we lose our ability to positively impact an outcome. I've learned, however, that it's not wise to let optimism alone influence goals.

Hope Is Not a Strategy

I'm an upbeat person who regularly encourages others to be positive and never give up hope. According to my family, friends and employees, I'm also unrealistic. Basing my business strategies on hope is shortsighted and potentially ill-fated. My long-term strategic plan needs to be more grounded so my leadership team can determine an ambitious, yet plausible direction.

> Before making changes and charting a new direction, be cautious and defensive.

It's been hard work, but I've broken some bad habits. I'm more practiced now at realistic thinking and have trained myself to view every situation in a more well-rounded manner. Successful people tend to think positively and creatively, but may fail to see problems rationally or from a negative perspective. When this occurs, they can miscalculate the opposition and neglect to prepare alternate plans. Before making changes and charting a new direction, move cautiously and defensively. Determining the weak and strong points sanctions you to eliminate, alter or prepare contingencies. In my own pursuits, I've grown so accustomed to thinking positively and forging right on ahead that I'm often blind to potential pitfalls, leaving me under-prepared for complications.

> It isn't in your best interest when natural optimism drives a plan.

I have much to learn. My wife, Diane—a logical, realistic thinker—reminded me of that recently. At our annual meeting for Steve Gilliland, Inc., we discussed the forecast and budget for the impending year. Centered on the launch of a new division of our company, I believed we would rapidly outgrow our current office space; therefore, we needed to adopt a more aggressive budget to expand our square footage. Our CFO (Diane), however, disagreed. It isn't in your best interest when natural optimism drives a financial plan, she proposed. She wanted a realistic revenue forecast for the new company and insisted that a 10-year commitment to office space needed to be based on projected revenue, marketing expenses and staffing. Nothing can dampen pie-in-the-sky enthusiasm like details, but she was absolutely right. We discussed worst-case scenarios and all agreed that we needed to postpone office expansion for the next two years. Because of Diane's savvy and ability to bring me back to earth, our company remains financially sound.

Define What You Value

According to Merriam-Webster, a person or thing's worth is the value they have when measured by their qualities or the esteem in which they are held. In essence, measuring the importance of things is an entirely subjective exercise based on one's own personal value system. As we confront new things and new situations, our evaluations must mature. When prevailing enticements mitigate values, reality is compromised. For example, I appreciated the camaraderie I established with a friend because she has a quality I admire:

passion. One day I discovered that she had lied to my wife about something. This prompted me to pit one value (passion) against another (honesty). Having decided that honesty is a higher value to me, I questioned her sincerity and the authenticity of our friendship.

> # Without truth there is no reality.

As a result of the conflict with this friend, I seized the occasion to revisit my values and, most importantly, outline their order. I simply asked myself, "How does this person fit into my hierarchy of values and do those values align with my position of what is important?" For me, an open heart, unconditional love and genuineness were at the top of my list. My ability to experience and create joy within my family took precedence over what I own, how I look, what clothes I wear, the car I drive and how much money is in my bank account. From my attitude regarding material possessions to how I devote my discretionary time away from my career, I did a thorough appraisal of what I regarded to be important. I concluded that without truth there is no reality. As I assessed that friendship, I quickly realized that on too many junctures I was sacrificing a higher value for a lesser one. I found myself defending my beliefs, succumbing to awkward settings and, on occasion, even agreeing to not disagree. Consequently, I found the worth of our friendship to have a fading return on my disbursement of time and energy.

Be True to Yourself

The 1960s hippie counterculture movement involved a variety of social concerns and beliefs. The hippies' primary tenet was that life was about being happy, not about what others thought you should be. It may be a little "hippie-like," but I believe you can do so much more with your life if you stay true to yourself. It takes only a few choices that align with what you desire to convince yourself that this is a beautiful way to live. When you finally choose to be your true self, there will be less stress, more understanding, less frustration and more compassion. You will set yourself on a path that can truly transform the way you experience this life. There's only one you in this world, so don't conceal or fake that. Embrace yourself.

> If you realize you've got a negative relationship with a supposed friend, maybe it's time to let that person go.

In our friendships, we sometimes abandon ourselves and our desires in small ways. It starts with a little critical self-talk, a judgmental reaction to someone, and moves right into some mean-spirited gossip about a so-called "friend." While these are small impediments from our true selves and, in most cases, don't make a big difference, they can snowball into long gossip sessions and a judgmental attitude towards others. We soon lose ourselves, our core. If you begin to feel this way, react differently next time and make that the first step in a new, learned behavior. Once you regularly choose what feels best and right for you, it becomes habit. True friends who display authenticity and genuineness will embrace the true you, flaws and all, and will help shape you to become a better person. In my own life, I am becoming more selective of who I consider a friend. I would rather have four quarters than 100 pennies. The people who love me don't need me to keep up appearances; they just appreciate who I am.

Don't change yourself just to fit into a group. You will be a better friend and can do so much more with your life if you stay true to your nature. If you realize you've got a negative relationship with a supposed friend, maybe it's time to let that person go. Not only would this remove a hurting relationship from your life, but he or she might afterward consider making personal changes. Such changes are entirely up to them, however, not you. Control what you can control.

It's All About You

If staying true to yourself becomes daunting, it can be easy to start giving your power away to others. You want their validation. You want them to tell you you're doing great. You want them to give you a path. Putting your trust in someone else, though, means you don't want to be responsible for what happens in your life. This is disempowering. Building genuine friendships, a fulfilling life and self-esteem are difficult if you're always trying to please everyone. Ultimately, your opinion of yourself is the only thing that should be able to make or break your day, your mood, your drive or your self-image. Just accept that some people are bound to dislike you and that it's nobody's fault.

> You're either going to spend time trying to be you or trying to hide yourself.

How many of your high school friendships have lasted through college and beyond? Not many, I'd bet. How many of us can honestly say that we're the same person today that we were at sixteen? Looking back, I feel kind of ridiculous remembering how I thought I needed to play sports in order to be cool. Moreover, I felt like a total loser when my conservative fundamental Baptist mother did not permit me to attend the high school dances. At the time, I was convinced my life was ruined.

Popularity fades after high school. An element of college that I loved was that no one person seemed to be popular. People were more accepting of each other's differences. It's time to move beyond that high school mentality and stop living by how others define you. You're either going to spend time trying to be you or trying to hide yourself. You can't do both. As Eleanor Roosevelt once said, "Do what you feel in your heart to be right—for you'll be criticized anyways." Once I realized life wasn't about being what I thought everyone else wanted me to be, I was finally able to be myself and find someone who loves every bit of it. So don't apologize for being yourself—it's all about you.

Open Your Heart

Opening your heart is an ongoing process that leads to clearer vision. It allows you to comprehend that, which is beyond your own understanding. In this open state, we are more likely to find lasting solutions to difficult problems. Dealing with others who act in ways I struggle to avoid is a big challenge for me. More often than not, I close my heart in situations where I feel threatened or could be hurt. Yet, hurt is part of the package when opening your heart. Although you risk losing comfort, self-esteem or material well-being, it isn't worth hardening your heart.

> You will learn more from failure than from success.

When your heart is open, you have the ability to love. While love can be perplexing, arduous, vexing and elusive, it magnifies awareness beyond yourself and unites you with a larger reality that seems to stretch into eternity. Closing your heart intensifies resentment towards someone or something and reduces your ability to ever find the essence of yourself and your true being. Part of being human means probing for answers to our problems, but that search can intensify the kinds of emotions that stimulate additional trouble. Granted, you will learn more from failure than from success; however, focusing solely on the negative will get you nowhere. Dwelling creates fear, further distancing you from the solution. Regardless of the detour, it is important to open your heart and unearth every possible course. Albert Einstein said,

"Problems cannot be solved at the same level of awareness that created them."

A Dose of Reality

I read about a frail old man who went to live with his son, daughter-in-law and four-year-old grandson. The old man's hands trembled, his eyesight was blurred, and his step faltered. The family ate together at the table, but the elder's shaky hands and failing sight made eating difficult. Peas rolled off his spoon and onto the floor. When he grasped his glass, milk spilled onto the tablecloth. The son and daughter-in-law became irritated with the mess. "We have to do something about Father," said the husband. "I've had enough of his spilled milk, noisy eating and food on the floor." So, they set a small table in the corner. There, the old man ate alone while the rest of the family enjoyed dinner. Since Grandfather had broken a dish or two, his food was served in a wooden bowl. As he sat alone, he sometimes had a tear in his eye. Still, the only words the couple had for him were sharp admonitions when he dropped a fork or spilled food. The four-year-old watched it all in silence.

> There is nothing like staring reality in the face to make a person recognize the need for change.

One evening, before supper, the father noticed his son playing with wood scraps on the floor. He asked the child sweetly, "What are you making?" Just as sweetly, the boy responded, "Oh, I am making a little bowl for you and Mama to eat your food in when I grow up." The four-year-old smiled and went back to work. The words so struck the parents that they were speechless. Then tears started to stream down their cheeks. There is nothing like staring reality in the face to make a person recognize the need for change. Though no word was spoken, both knew what must be done. That evening, the husband took Grandfather's hand and gently led him back to the family table. For the remainder of his days he ate every meal with them. Regrettably, many of us realize value only after it is seen from another's perspective.

You're Only Human

We all make mistakes, but that doesn't mean we should have to pay for them the rest of our lives. Sometimes good people make bad choices. It doesn't mean we're bad—it means we're human. To see things as they really are, be aware of and accepting of the humanness in yourself and in others. Awareness gives you the power to choose what kind of person you are. The challenge is to accept both the positive and the negative aspects of yourself. Sometimes you just have to shut up, swallow your pride and accept that you're human. It's called growing up, not giving up. The late Maya Angelou used to say, "Most people don't grow up. Most people age. They find parking spaces, honor their credit cards, get married, have children and call that maturity. What that is, is aging."

> Mistakes represent
> huge opportunities for
> self-improvement.

Growing up may not seem exciting when you're actually in the process. But when you look back, even the biggest detour will seem like a warmhearted memory. The day you realized your parents weren't perfect, you became an adolescent. The day you realized they were human and forgave them, you became an adult. What distinguishes a virtuous person from a dishonest one is candidly admitting to a mistake and taking the steps necessary to rectify them. When we make a mistake, we face a choice about what to do. Ignoring it makes us feel better in the short term, but increases the likelihood that we'll repeat it. Our best option is to discover why we made the mistake and then become better. That's how we grow. Mistakes represent huge opportunities for self-improvement. Life is about the way you see it, the way someone else sees it and the way it really is.

Discover Your Blind Spots

From childhood on into adulthood, we tend to believe what we hear. Many of our spiritual beliefs are formed early in life when we hear things for the first time. We accept them as truths, just like we do the existence of rocks and trees and the other tangibles in nature. We carry these opinions our whole lives unless we dig deeper. We consider these beliefs to be factual and deem ourselves invulnerable to the biases that influence other people. Consequently, when we hear something counter to our beliefs, we react not as though someone is sharing an opinion, but as though they are denying reality. The flaw is in them, we decide, not us.

> ## Our blind spots will detach us from reality.

Unbeknownst to us, we have psychological blind spots that threaten to harm our relationships with others. Although it's generally not pleasant to confront these aspects of ourselves, it's necessary to address and acknowledge these annoying habits. The most conventional way to find them is to ask the people closest to you for some honest feedback about your strengths and weaknesses. Asking can be difficult, of course, and, if those people aren't totally honest for fear of hurting your feelings, it really serves no purpose. For me, a simpler method is to analyze my reaction to a trait in someone else. When I react negatively, it could signal that I possess the trait myself and that it's time to do something about it. The bottom line is that our blind spots will detach us from reality. Whether we act on our own or with the help of others, uncovering blind spots is an important step in uncovering another side of the story.

I Love You, You're Perfect, Now Change

The musical *I Love You, You're Perfect, Now Change* premiered Off-Broadway at the Westside Theatre on August 1, 1996 and closed on July 27, 2008, after 5,003 performances. I attended 3 of those. The play's tagline inspired me: "Everything you have ever secretly thought about dating, romance, marriage, lovers, husbands, wives and in-laws, but were afraid to admit." It would become one of my all-time favorite shows because of the brilliant and clever manner in which it presented an overall arc to relationships throughout the course of one's life. A play pitting truth against reality, it revealed the contradictory nature of beliefs and relationships.

> Embrace what you want and release what you don't.

For me, it was more than a play. At the time, as a single father of two boys, it was a chance to escape and reminisce about my past, reflect about my present and dream about my future. The production served as a catalyst to my recognizing that change is unavoidable. Now, here I sit writing a book about change with a working title of *Detour*. The biggest lesson I learned from *I Love You, You're Perfect, Now Change* was we choose who, what and how we will be in each moment. With a heavy dose of humor, it suggested that as we change, our relationships change. What jolted me was the theme "embrace what you want and release what you don't." That, my friends, takes courage! However, that is your responsibility. Break old habits and release yourselves from relationships that no longer serve you. Yes, I confess that all three times I left the Westside Theater in New York I was laughing and crying at the same time; however, I was also repeating the mantra over and over again in my mind: *You cannot control others, but you can control yourself.*

The Truth About the Truth

Winston Churchill said, "Men stumble over the truth, but most pick themselves up and hurry off as if nothing has happened." To develop the mindset of reality, get comfortable with the truth and face up to it. It doesn't matter how sound your thinking is if it's based on assumption. Reality can't be found in the absence of facts or in the presence of poor information. Nothing beats fully examining the pros and cons before plunging ahead. Finding reality means pursuing the truth and admitting to your deficiencies. If you haven't developed a mindset of reality, maybe you need a robust prescription of the truth. Ask your best friend, spouse, coworker, neighbor and children to write down your three greatest strengths and weaknesses. Don't defend yourself. Just pay attention. You are only allowed to ask questions that help you understand their choices. Spend a day examining yourself in light of what you've learned: "Mirror, mirror, on the wall, is this really me?"

> The truth can set you free,
> but chances are it will
> first make you angry.

We grew up being taught that there are two sides to every story. I would argue there are actually three: the way you see it, the way someone else sees it and the way it really is. Our emotions and experience sometimes don't permit us to see another's point of view. Our opinions often can't be swayed, which is fine if we have all the facts. Yet, how many of us base our opinions on conjecture? Worse is basing our opinions on what other people think instead of making informed decisions. We decide what would be the more popular, accepted choice instead of what we honestly know to be true.

It has been suggested that some of today's media, in fanning the flames of debate instead of presenting facts, has created a fourth side of the story that doesn't align with one side or the other or even represent the truth. What is real, then, when opinions, biases and agendas are added to the mix? Truth becomes almost impossible to sift out. When an investigator interviews several people who witnessed the same incident, they often find that no one is intentionally lying. Recall varies depending on the person's perspective. In your mind, you try to piece together a puzzle that accurately depicts the reality of what you've just seen. Depending on the situation, walls are built, judgments are made, and opinions are formed. I hear your side, you hear mine, and we walk away leaving truth unattended.

The truth can set you free, but chances are it will first make you angry. As you confront the detours in life that knock you off course, remember that the perceived reality of any moment is influenced by a great many factors. It is vital for us to peel away bias, distraction and ulterior motives to even attempt to fully understand what is true. There are three sides to every story, yes, but there is only one freeing truth.

"I want you to put me in touch with reality, but be ready to break the connection *fast.*"

4

THE MINDSET OF
RESOURCEFULNESS

Dismissing the Self-Imposed Limitations

re·source·ful·ness

ri- ˈsȯrs-fəl-nis/

noun

1. the quality of being able to cope with a difficult situation. Capable of devising ways and means.

2. a source of aid or support that may be drawn upon when needed.

A Tough Pill to Swallow

When I ask people what they want out of life, I often hear a litany of things they don't want instead. Where focus goes, so goes energy. If you continually focus on what you don't want, you'll end up only with what you settle for. From the top down, many of us list our priorities according to the paths of least resistance. That's declaring failure before you even get started. These limitations are entirely self-imposed. We don't want to hear that because it's a tough pill to swallow.

> If you're running east looking for a sunset, it doesn't matter how committed you are.

Such an approach protects you from failure and the pain associated with it, but at the expense of growth and fulfillment. Make sure what you're doing is leading where you really want to go. If you're running east looking for a sunset, it doesn't matter how committed you are. Until you realize that some of your actions are based on learned behavior, not reality, you may find yourself stuck in an imaginary, self-imposed rut. You can rid yourself of the associated fear, shame, guilt and humiliation when you finally stop doubting yourself and being afraid to make a mistake. Each of us is capable of far more than we typically give ourselves credit for. Genuine success is about stepping beyond self-imposed limitations to create the quality of life you truly seek.

Behavior Changes Feelings

Yes, overcoming self-imposed limitations can be very challenging and require sacrifices. It means a change in attitude and feelings, taking action and a change in mindset, too. Behavior alters feelings. In other words, do something about cleaning the garage and you'll feel better about the garage. Make a conscious effort to be more patient with people and you'll feel better about yourself. With so much in the world seemingly beyond our control, it's a shame when we don't pursue things that actually are controllable. I am not referring to legitimate obstacles all of us face from time to time regarding finance, health and work commitments, but some things just aren't realistic given our DNA. I don't have the athleticism of Michael Jordan or the vocal chops of Josh Groban, for instance, no matter how much I might like to imagine. That doesn't mean I can't enjoy shooting hoops or singing my heart out. I am referring to the self-imposed limitations that keep us from accomplishing things to which we aspire. Instead of using the time, talent and mental and physical capacity God gave us, we hurt ourselves when we ignore our inner yearnings by making excuses.

> Challenge your assumptions so you can experience new things that might turn out to be one-time pleasures or lifelong satisfactions.

As a die-hard Steelers fan, I often hear someone say, "I would love to go to Pittsburgh and see a game at Heinz Field, but I've never been able to." Invariably, the reason they can't is because they won't—meaning there's nothing really stopping them other than their own inability to turn desire into action. Usually, the "never been able to" gets back to their sense that somehow this is just a dream and they aren't willing to take the steps or make the sacrifices necessary to fulfill it. Challenge your assumptions so you can experience new things that might turn out to be one-time pleasures or lifelong satisfactions. If you don't like Chinese food because you've never tasted it, try it. If you tasted it once, try it again until you find a dish you like. (Least you think I'm being overly critical, this is really about me! I've denied myself access to an incredible world simply because I've stubbornly refused to try something different or step outside my comfort zone.) Whether you're missing out on things due to indecisiveness, low self-esteem, risk aversion, lack of confidence, laziness or stress about change, it's essential to realize that many of your boundaries are self-induced—and, therefore, surmountable.

Make an Anxiety Appointment

It's one thing to believe you can accomplish something, an entirely different matter to actually schedule an exact date and time to do it. Some say that believing is the first step to overcoming self-imposed limits. I contend that belief comes only after you have made a commitment and started working towards a task you've avoided. I have asked numerous employees and thousands of people who have heard me speak these questions: "What would you try to achieve if you knew for certain that you wouldn't fail?" Then, "What's the worst that could happen if you took on this challenge and failed?" Your own answers will reveal the depth of your anxieties—as long as you are truthful. As author Steven Pressfield said, "The more afraid you are of something, the more resistance you will feel."

> ## Preparation nurtures confidence.

Back in 1999, I scared myself to death. I had a secure job that provided an attractive salary, incredible benefits and an ideal retirement package—and I was contemplating giving it all up. What scared me most was knowing the direction I wanted to be moving towards and recognizing that my reluctance was entirely self-inflicted. I expended way too much energy dwelling on my fear when what I really needed to do was focus on tackling the challenge. So I started to prepare for my lifelong dream of becoming an author and speaker. The more I prepared myself for the transition, the more my confidence grew. I was chipping away at my fear, despite encountering some unexpected obstacles (detours!) along the way. One crucial step was enlisting the support of others to keep me on track and hold me accountable. As my former secretary Margaret always said, "The day you wake up and your life is directed by sole sovereignty is the same day you'll make some major missteps."

> Ending self-imposed
> limitations starts with
> expressing what worries you
> the most and purposefully
> opposing your fears.

Not until I made an anxiety appointment (i.e., turning in my resignation) did I experience what, today, my family and friends realize was life changing for me. Sharing my struggles and pursuits with others was an important step in the process. The temptation to succumb to your self-imposed limits is far greater if you pursue your ambitions without a support system. I've always said that the ride is more enjoyable when you know where you're going and when the car is full of people you care about.

If you don't challenge yourself, you won't grow. Simple as that. Ending self-imposed limitations starts with expressing what worries you the most and purposefully opposing those fears. Remember, there is nothing and no one holding you back but yourself.

So, what will your next test be?

Develop Yourself Through Reflection

Through the years, I have become a better communicator, developed self-awareness, built self-confidence and learned quickly from my mistakes by regularly recording my thoughts, feelings and experiences. I have shared with many audiences that the formula for me in writing a book is to revisit the journaling I have done through the years. Journaling has helped me to reflect on the mistakes I've made and on how to avoid them in the future. It's also helped me to develop my critical thinking and problem-solving skills—not to mention become more self-aware and emotionally mature. As part of requiring all of my leadership team to read the book Scaling Up, I also advocated they keep a journal of what they were learning. For a few, that sounded like a waste of effort, especially when it'd be just another thing to fit into an already busy schedule. However, the results were noteworthy. Journaling helped them develop communication skills by expressing feelings more clearly and forcing them to write more often.

> No matter how lousy your day was, try reflecting on at least one positive thing that happened.

Shravan Goli, President of Dictionary.com, believes that, in the world of business, students will need good, solid reading and writing skills. Goli states, "I'm a little worried about where we are in America with literacy levels dropping. Are these electronic devices helping us or making it worse?" No matter whether or not you believe cyber slang is damaging students' writing acumen, the fact is that journaling has been proven to help people deal with negative events more effectively. One key study showed that people who used a journal to describe and analyze their emotions after a stressful event felt more positive about it in the long term. This is not even remotely suggesting that you should use social media as an arena for venting negative emotions. When a detour occurs, journaling allows you to vent positively—as long as you don't lash out at people who have nothing to do with the source of your frustration. Try not to sugarcoat your day. Be honest about what you thought, how you acted or how a person made you feel. No matter how lousy your day was, try reflecting on at least one positive thing that happened. For me, I always come back to thinking about things I am grateful for, such as my health, my skills and family. It's too easy to take things for granted if you're having a bad time.

A Jury of One

At some point in our lives, we all feel guilty about something. Whether your guilt will help you or break you depends largely on what you choose to focus on. You can either focus on what you've lost or what you've done wrong, or you can shift your attention towards a desired outcome. If something is causing you a lot of guilt, make a commitment to work towards the desired goal attached to it. For many, that's a feeling of unbearable guilt and shame for having wasted time. Often in our lives, we stop and think about where we stand, how much ground we have covered and what we have done so far. We compare our progress to others and where we had expected we'd be. We create a self-imposed detour when we realize we haven't done enough and see the missed opportunities due to our carelessness and complacency. This can induce an overwhelming sense of guilt and despair and stimulate destructive feelings.

> Guilt can have only as much power over you as you allow it.

The sooner you feel in control, the sooner the pain will dissipate. Stop beating yourself up about guilt. You don't have to answer to a jury of your peers. The good thing about guilt is that it indicates where your desires lie, revealing what you need to do to feel happier. Just because you wasted time and wavered a few times doesn't mean you can't turn this feeling around and use it as a motivator. For those of you reading this book who don't know my whole story, maybe I should insert a reminder. I was thirty-nine years old and feeling more guilt than I had ever imagined. As a result of my divorce, my mother, brother and everyone who was a part of my life, disappeared for a period of time. My mother was disappointed in where I had landed because of my choices, and my brother was more or less blissfully content with my circumstance. I was an embarrassment to my family, and my "so called" friends were all gone. Not until I decided to take the necessary steps to move in a different direction did I stop feeling bad and do something about it. Because of my guilt, I experienced remarkable growth. I can't even describe the freedom I felt. Remember, guilt can have only as much power over you as you allow it. It's never too late to turn things around. Never. You might feel like you can't make up the time you've wasted, but I am living proof that you can, indeed, make positive changes in your life and be happy.

Decide to Do More

Author William Arthur Ward said, "Do more than belong—participate." There are three types of people in this world: those who make things happen, those who watch things happen and those who wonder what happened. To successfully navigate life's turns, be that person who makes things happen. All too many of us have replaced the "I will do more" mentality with "I've fallen and I can't get up." Why? Often, the attention we receive by not getting up and then complaining about it seems more attractive than persevering with no one noticing. When you live your life on the sidelines, you never risk having someone criticize or ridicule your intentions. Life is too short for misgivings. If you get a chance to do more, take it, regardless of whether or not you'll be recognized. If it changes your life, let it. Doing more isn't necessarily easy, but it's well worth the effort!

- Do more than belong—participate
- Do more than care—help
- Do more than believe—practice
- Do more than be fair—be kind
- Do more than be friendly—be a friend
- Do more than forgive—forget

- Do more than dream—work

- Do more than teach—inspire

- Do more than earn—enrich

- Do more than live—grow

When you resolve to do more, a surprising and energizing result materializes. You find that life's detours are less common and the challenges you encounter are easier to cope with. Resourcefulness is more than imagination or originality. It is an eagerness to participate and, in the process, help other people navigate their own twists and opportunities.

Fly Below the Radar

Everyone knows at least one. I'm talking about the person who needs all eyes on them at all times. If you can't think of that person, you may be that person. These people find a reasonable amount of success professionally, or so they say. According to them, there's nothing they don't have. Their Facebook posts are never dull and always sound extravagant. Instead of telling you they found a great sweater at Marshalls, they say, "Nordstrom's is having a sale with my name on it." They don't drive a car, they drive a brand. They are movers and shakers, and the people they associate with should consider themselves lucky to spend time with them. Sadly, whenever you encounter someone flying straight into the radar and acting a bit on the extreme side, you can wager that he or she is compensating for something on the not-so-self-assured side. Some adults strive for attention and will pay any price just to get it. They create self-induced boundaries when they believe they are fashioning conduits to more opportunities. They have an insincere sense of privilege, which manifests itself in jealousy, arrogance and overconfidence.

> Love the people who treat you right and forget the ones who don't.

Psychologists might say such people are overcompensating for being neglected as children, that they lack self-worth while appearing to brim with self-assurance. One consequence of such behavior can be not having true friendships or any kind of relationship built on equivalence. If, on the other hand, you fly below the radar, you're more likely to hear more, see more and learn more. You're more inclined to love the people who treat you right and forget the ones who don't. When people who use or mistreat you step away from your life, don't run after them.

Create Your Trademark

Have you ever considered all of the ways you sabotage yourself? Unhealthy habits, self-doubt, self-judgments, gossip, procrastination and other behaviors inhibit you from coping with changes that could positively affect your life. Have you ever thought about the person you would like to become—the person you know may be diametrically opposed to your parents' underlying beliefs, but whom you know is better adjusted. Are you happy with your relationships, work and life style? Are your relationships genuine? Is your work fulfilling, and is your life style built for you or for someone else? What are the priorities that would bring you more inner peace, well-being and fulfillment? Question your motives, ideas and assumptions about who you are and how you make others feel.

> When you become the
> architect of your life,
> you remain free.

Questioning our viewpoint, mindset and assumptions brings us closer to sensible mindfulness. When you become the architect of your life, you remain free. My mother-in-law, Rita Rohde, is the symbol of autonomy and independence. Since 1960, she has had 34 surgeries, including 6 hip replacements. She has never felt like she was caught in a trap. Her mindset of resourcefulness is an example to every person who complains and plays the role of the victim. Rita not only embraces change, she changes the perceptions of people around her. Her positive outlook is a testimony to everyone who knows her. She has enriched the lives of her friends, neighbors and family by seeing beyond her present circumstances. Her attitude has inspired hope in the face of adversity and order during disarray. She never makes excuses. She just smiles and conveys calmness in spite of her physical trials. Your smile is your logo, your personality is your business card, and how others feel after spending time with you is your trademark. While Coca-Cola has a secret recipe and a prevailing brand that has never been replicated, Rita has created a trademark that is available to any person willing to question their motives and take a hard look at how they make other people feel.

Make Uniqueness Your Clique

Have you ever awakened on a Saturday morning, jumped in the car and taken an unplanned road trip? When is the last time you actually veered off course on purpose? For every person who confines themselves to the lines in a coloring book, there are those who believe that coloring outside of them gives the drawing more pizzazz. When someone says, "You can't," they are revealing their limitations, not yours. In my book *Enjoy The Ride*, I challenge people to be different. Many alienate themselves from change because they revel in the comfort of being average. They arrange their lives into familiar patterns, proud to follow in the proverbial footsteps set before them and secure in the knowledge that they are part of a large group of people just like them. The clique mentality that appealed to them in their youth now harbors reassurance in their adulthood.

> Leave the cliques to those who need them.

If familiar patterns bore you and, perchance, you do not prefer the company of people with whom everyone presumes you should identify, then be prepared for adversity. Trailblazers don't worry about how many people agree with them—rather, how many people might profit from their nerve. I have always championed the side of "I did it my way" instead of "I might not be accepted." When you spend your life trying to fit in, you risk not meeting interesting and fascinating people. There are many distinctive people whose minds don't function like yours does. That's okay! Blending in doesn't always work, so don't take it personally. Leave the cliques to those who need them. I've met folks who claim they have a lot of friends when, in actuality, they merely entertain a lot of vague connections or acquaintances. Once I recognized that cliques could be damaging to the spirit of those who don't "fit in" and that some members in a clique don't play well with others, I happily detached myself from such circles.

Bet on Yourself

If you were a stock, would you bet on yourself? As you ponder your answer, you will undoubtedly ask yourself some other questions. Am I talented? Am I worthy? Am I capable? Do you believe in your own potential so sincerely and unequivocally that you would make that investment over buying shares in Apple? You know what you are worth. When you encounter a detour, how do you see your value and potential then? If the question gives you pause, you have some work to do. What's holding you back? What have you done lately to improve your skill set and make your stock rise? Just like athletes, at some point you may become a free agent in your personal and professional life. While I would wish that every person reading this book would end up joyfully married to the same person their entire lives and could choose a vocation that could last forever, statistics say otherwise.

> The new generations of employees are no longer remaining loyal to a firm they know has no loyalty to them.

As the workplace continues to evolve and relationships become more complex, loyalty will continue to be an issue. The biggest change in the workplace will be the employee/employer relationship. Employee loyalty comes down to the actions of the more dominant side of the equation, which is the company. I hear a lot of people say, "Today's generation of employees just doesn't care about the long-term." At times, I have been considered naïve, but I don't think humanity has changed that much. Since the 1940s, people have wanted to be more in control of their lives. What's different now is how companies treat employees. The new generations of employees are no longer remaining loyal to a firm they know has no loyalty to them. You need to continually reinvent yourself. I'm sure you've heard this ad nauseam, but you really do have to believe in your own abilities or no one else will. Love your skill set, your vision and yourself. Self-confidence isn't ambiguous or unstructured. Recognize your gifts and talents.

Own them and hone them. Invest in yourself until you feel others would be willing to do the same. Whether you're in the market for a new career or a new relationship, it's time to raise the value of your stock!

Faith, Family and Friends

Economists and psychologists have been studying happiness for a long time. It turns out that, according to twin studies at the University of Minnesota, happiness depends on genetics in some very important ways. So, just like the advice given to world-class marathoners, choose your parents well! ☺

But there are also important ways in which our choices affect our happiness. In a recent *New York Times* article, Arthur Brooks, an economist at the American Enterprise Institute, wrote that there are four things affecting individual happiness that we have direct control over: faith, family, community/friends and work.

> One of the greatest assets we can have in coping with demanding circumstances is controlling and continually improving our family/life balance.

When life's roadblocks and detours seem never-ending, and when you find yourself stressing at work or rushing from place to place in a mad frenzy, don't forget to keep in touch with these three pillars of sanity: faith, family and friends. Even as I continue to work hard and remain thankful for all I have been blessed with in this life, I constantly remind myself that my most cherished experiences revolve around those three gifts. When I attend a pro football game, what I treasure most isn't the food, the souvenirs or the outcome—it's the laughter, smiles and memories of being together. One of the greatest assets we can have in coping with demanding circumstances is controlling and continually improving our family/life balance. When challenges confront you, you'll always have something to fall back on.

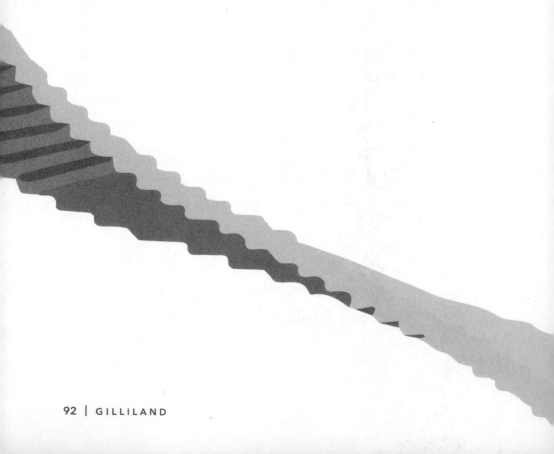

Resourceful Considerations

The world is changing at its fastest rate in history. Standing still means being left behind. If you can't adapt, you'll lose control. It's natural to seek stability and certainty. Resourcefulness means stepping outside your present condition to achieve what you desire. While your aspirations may never change, the path to realizing them almost certainly will. Here are five final considerations.

- ✓ Learn to say "I want."

    Identifying and articulating what you want is the catalyst for getting it.

- ✓ Live from the inside out.

    Don't get caught up in doing what you think you should do because of outside influences. Do what you really want, which originates from the inside.

- ✓ Increase your options.

    Once you recognize that you need others to help you, and that looking and asking for help is not a weakness, you open up a world of greater possibility.

- ✓ Learn from others.

    The situation you are facing has happened before or been experienced by someone, somewhere, at some time. Learn from the knowledge of others.

- ✓ Prepare hard.

    Relaxed awareness is a state of mind that helps put aside apprehension. Preparation creates a calm consciousness so your brain can work at what it does best—looking after you.

5

THE MINDSET OF
RECEPTIVENESS

Choosing the Belief of Possibilities

re·cep·tive·ness

ri-ˈsep-tiv-nis

noun

1. tending to receive new ideas
    or suggestions favorably.

2. willingness or readiness to receive
    (especially impressions or ideas).

Chickens Don't Lay Eggs Benedict

My wife, Diane, is a great cook. When I come home after a long road trip, I always look forward to the smell of spicy aromas that promise a tasty feast. Not only does she know how to prepare a meal, but she's also a master at presentation. She is the definition of a gourmet chef. The colors of the food on the plate, beautifully arranged in harmony with meat, rice pilaf and a vegetable casserole, welcome me home. But the food was not so attractive before she got her hands on it. The meat was raw, the rice was brittle, and the vegetables needed scrubbed and trimmed. The process of receptiveness requires a similar progression. You begin by taking your raw ability and a willingness to blend it over time with various acquired skill sets and people who can help you transform your life in a way you imagined. When people say, "I wish I could cook like you," what they are really acknowledging is that they are not as willing as you are to try new things. Another thing I have heard from a family member is, "I could never afford that." What they are actually admitting is that they would love to have what I have, but they are not willing to work that hard to acquire it. For them, opportunity comes disguised as hard work.

> While success includes milestones, the emphasis is on the journey, not on the original destination.

We live in a world where premixed, precooked and fast have replaced fresh, sautéed and deliberate. The inclinations of the latest generations are to gravitate towards anything that is quick, easy and requires little obligation. Over the past few years, social researchers have noted that young adults are dating less. Instead, dating has been replaced by "hanging out." Generation Y and the Millennials aren't big on making commitments to people or to organizations while they try to find themselves. Instead of telling a person directly that you're interested in them by asking them on a date, you can now send "Crush" alerts on Facebook. The Internet has made connecting with people easier, but has also made us lazier at establishing meaningful relationships. Success in anything, even relationships, is a process—a mindset. While success includes milestones, the emphasis is on the journey, not on the original destination. There are no shortcuts to a great relationship, financial freedom or an incredible serving of Eggs Benedict. Despite the many changes that have provided us with simpler means to accomplish various undertakings, paying one's dues remains the most reliable option for nearly any pursuit.

Life Imparts Lessons

You can tell a lot about a person by the way he or she handles a rainy day, the elderly, lost luggage and tangled Christmas tree lights. One assurance we all have is that life comes with bumps. It requires alterations, compromises, strength, forgiveness, hopefulness, trust, love and patience. Fortunately, no matter what happens, how bad it seems today, life goes on, and tomorrow will offer a new start. Don't go through life with a catcher's mitt on both hands—you need to be able to throw back sometimes. I have learned firsthand that every detour can teach you many lessons—if you are open to all possibilities.

> Being aware of all available options can improve your chances of making smart choices.

What other gems have I learned along the way?

- Making a living is not the same thing as making a life.
- An unwise choice can ruin your life.
- Life gives you second chances.
- Knowing your values helps you make choices consistent with what's important.
- Being aware of all available options can improve your chances of making smart choices.
- If you pursue happiness, it will elude you. If you focus on family, friends, the needs of others, work and doing your very best, happiness will find you.
- Decisions made with an open heart are usually the right ones.
- Even when I'm in pain, I don't have to be one.
- And, most significantly, I still have a lot to learn!

Life Builds Character

We don't really pay attention, do we? Seems like we're always trying to finish things as quickly as possible, robbing us of the childlike wonder of focusing in on smaller details and asking, "Why is that there?" One good way to counteract that behavior is to identify the negative consequences of your rush to get things done, then develop constructive habits that force you to slow down.

> The journey is where our character, personality, passions and authentic self are revealed.

Imagine keeping your eyes closed for an entire trip. Unwittingly addicted to instant gratification, that is exactly what many of us do. We focus on the end result and the future while overlooking the path we took to get there. "So," you might ask, "what about setting goals?" Outlining clearly defined objectives instills hope, fuels ambition and gives us a sense of accomplishment, of course. The journey, however, is where our character, personality, passions and authentic self are revealed—where our innermost growth and strength are nurtured. Sadly, we have convinced ourselves that the finish line is king. The faster we can get there, the greater chance we have of avoiding pain, disappointment, mistakes and failure—of *winning*, however we define that. Every challenge I have faced, though, has made me emotionally healthier and stronger, so I've learned to appreciate those unanticipated "character builders" along the way.

Life Delivers Clues

The most insightful thing that happened to me is when I gently let go of the idea that I needed to be in control and figure everything out. I taught myself to embrace the notion that my only requirements in certain situations were to observe and enjoy. That's quite a challenge for a control freak. I have exhausted a ton of energy, effort and intensity directing stuff that doesn't need it. For instance, at tailgate parties, I'd tend to organize the food items on the table, the placement of chairs, the position of the grill and, on occasion, even park neighboring cars to fit within the gamut of what I believed was most befitting the occasion. I'd spend more time directing and agonizing than participating. Instead of enjoying myself, I felt stress (self-imposed stress, at that). When I realized that some of the greatest joys could be had without me lifting a finger or speaking a word, I began to more fully appreciate my environment. The more I observed, the more I learned.

> The more you observe, and the more accustomed you become to not trying to figure everything out, the more enjoyable life becomes.

When you look beyond your own agenda and start experiencing the magic of life, you actually see what is truly going on around you. You listen with awareness, watch with wonder and understand what is being communicated between words. You tune into opportunities and new levels of excitement. The more you observe, and the more accustomed you become to not trying to control everything, the more enjoyable life becomes. Thus, when unexpected detours arise, causing you to change course, you will be in a better frame of mind to react. Look back on your life. Didn't some of the greatest times you've had occur when you let go and just allowed things to happen? Isn't that what holidays are supposedly all about? All too often, we say, "Yeah, but there's so much to do!" Is that truly the case? Most likely, if you would cut back, ask for help, prioritize and let go, the ride would be more pleasurable. Observation allows you to distinguish between the doing and the being of life.

Life Provides Opportunities

After 20 children and 6 staff members were murdered in a Connecticut school in 2012, the entire nation was stunned. We focused on the tragedy and the questions surrounding it: What kind of person could do such a thing—and why? How can we prevent it from happening again? How can we help the survivors? Amid the chaos and all the unanswered questions, an unlikely group moved in and offered assistance. From Chicago came dogs—specially trained golden retrievers that offered nothing but affection. Dogs can't speak; they are simply present and attentive. Children traumatized by the violence opened up to them, expressing fears and emotions they had not spoken to any adult. As one dog trainer said, "The biggest part of their training is just learning to be still."

Too many times we miss an opportunity because we are broadcasting when should be tuning in.

More often than not, we are inclined to discard new ideas or anything different—which could explain why opportunities always look bigger going than coming. Instead of being receptive to a fresh approach, we cling to the old ways, then wonder why our frustrations mount. When you encounter a turn in the road that requires a change in your preset course, don't pigheadedly contest it. Embrace it.

Life doesn't come with guarantees or directions. What it offers are possibilities. Too many times we miss these opportunities because we're broadcasting when should be tuning in. Just like the golden retrievers that were specifically trained for comforting silence, we need to be receptive when faced with a detour. Success author Napoleon Hill said, "Opportunity often comes disguised in the form of misfortune or temporary defeat." In this frenetic society of ours, slow down and tune in. This isn't a practice life—it's the real deal. Give every detour its due. Rerouting isn't a bad thing when you're open to new possibilities and flexible enough to take advantage of the moment.

Temptation Is Not Opportunity

Opportunity may only knock once, but temptation leans on the doorbell. One of the biggest challenges you will face is when the magnetism of something, or someone, pulls you in a direction that can alter your life path forever. There is no right way to do a wrong thing. Every day, people try to validate their dishonest actions because of their situations. Right and wrong are not defined by our circumstances, but whether we do what is right or what is wrong defines who we are. Your biggest challenge will always be to do what is right, not what is easy. Detours sometimes invite us to veer off an absolute course because the facade of the new direction seems less restrictive. In 2001, the office supply superstore Staples introduced the Easy Button® as part of their rebranding effort, which ultimately became one of the most successful mass-marketing campaigns in recent memory. Our lives don't have an Easy Button®, however. We can't push a button and expect the results will be what we want.

> Unconscious, intuitive and instinctual reactions let you know immediately what choice is right.

Every day, you are faced with two options when it comes to making choices: easy vs. right. The right choice doesn't originate in your heart or head. It comes from your gut. Unconscious, intuitive and instinctual reactions let you know immediately which choice is right. So why do you choose otherwise? Because the right choice will often lead to the edge of your comfort zone. The easy choice tells a salesperson to take the rest of the day off after making a big sale in the morning. The right choice tells you to keep working and moving closer to your dreams. How many times have you devoured a huge meal and regretted it an hour later when you felt bloated and immobile? Yet, the next day, you overdo it again. The right thing would be to cut back on your portions and limit (or eliminate!) dessert. The easy choice gives you instant gratification despite your awareness of the consequences. Temptation causes you to choose based on opportunity, and such weakness becomes habit. Changing that habit takes grit, time and conscious effort. Don't expect a quick fix—and don't give up! The pursuit of any goal in life comes with options. The question you need to continually ask yourself is, "Will my choice get me closer to my dreams or farther away?" When faced with any important choice, remind yourself that temptation is a detour, not an opportunity.

Contentment Rejects Opportunities

Next time you see water streaming over rocks, notice how clean and clear it appears. Because it's constantly stirring, the water contains a lot of dissolved oxygen and thus becomes aerated. Next, take a peek at a stationery puddle that's been trapped within rocks and logs. Most likely, it'll be brownish and infused with algae and debris. Bacteria consume the dissolved oxygen from underneath. Drinkable water flows constantly; whereas, stagnant water has become polluted from inactivity.

Contentment, like all emotions, is transient. Oddly enough, we often think or hear that contentment is an admirable goal. Well, just as I've claimed in other books that a destination will always outdistance us and therefore can't be attained, I am now advocating that we should not pursue contentment either.

> When you succumb to the comfort of stringent daily routines, you are avoiding growth or change.

Contentment, when defined as "this is as good as it's going to get, so I'd better stick to the same thing," is like the puddle of stagnant water. Although it's fun and relaxing to sit on the couch and chill out, when did this become the only reward for working hard? Is that truly contentment, though? When you succumb to the comfort of stringent daily routines, you are avoiding growth or change. You stagnate. After several years of this, you could still be looking at your spouse, friends, neighbors, meals or house in the exact same way, never having made any changes and having stopped growing out of fear or torpor. Can you say midlife crisis? When you shun new things and fool yourself into thinking you are content, monotony will ultimately set in. No matter your age, your higher self yearns for change and growth. Even the slightest variation in routine can make a difference. When you realize you've become inactive, wade into the water, get in up to your waist and then dive under. Contentment can cause you to miss out on new discoveries and passions for life that come with receptiveness.

Get Beyond Your Assumptions

We're involuntarily programmed. We can hear the same message on a regular basis and rarely (or never) expose ourselves to alternatives. Accustomed to such patterns, we become far more likely to accept what we hear without thinking. To escape your narrow box, surround yourself with a spectrum of information rather than simply settling for the message that makes you feel most comfortable. Here's a news flash: the world changes! Yesterday's common sense is today's backward thinking. A century ago, a cultural imprint went something like this: "Cars will never take off. They require pavement, and who'll pay to pave an entire downtown when there are so few cars around to use such roads?" Sometimes, conventional wisdom simply becomes obsolete. "Customers will never buy water in bottles when they can get it free from the tap."

> The less you know about an opportunity, the more attractive it is.

Find freedom beyond your assumptions in order to foster innovation, creativity and thinking outside the box. I have challenged so many people in my personal and professional life to at least try some alternatives. Instead of following the herd, make sure you're in touch with reality. You will begin to learn how much of your life is *group* thinking rather than *you* thinking. Yes, it can be scary, but it might open your eyes to a whole new world of opportunity. The less you know about an opportunity, the more attractive it is. When you go against the norm, you will hear that inner voice of self-doubt, criticism and fear. To repel small and negative thoughts, reconnect with the bigger vision and purpose of your life. You are younger today than you ever will be again, so make the best use of it.

Don't Jump to Conclusions

A man sat at a Metro station in Washington, DC and started to play the violin. It was a cold January morning. He played six Bach pieces for about 45 minutes. During that time—rush hour—an estimated 1,100 people went through the station, most of them on their way to work. Three minutes went by, and a middle-aged man noticed there was a musician playing. He slowed his pace, stopped for a few seconds and then hurried up to meet his schedule. A minute later, the violinist received his first dollar tip: a woman threw the money in the till and, without stopping, hurried on. A few minutes later, someone leaned against the wall to listen, but soon looked at his watch and headed off again. Clearly, he was late for work. The one who paid the most attention was a 3-year-old boy. His mother dragged him along hurriedly, but the kid stopped to look at the violinist. Finally, the mother pushed more urgently, and the child continued with her, turning his head back the whole time. Several other children repeated this action. All of the parents, without exception, urged them on. In the 45 minutes the musician played, only half a dozen people lingered attentively. About 20 left him money, but continued on at their normal pace. The musician collected $32. When he finished playing, no one seemed to notice the transition from music to silence. No one applauded, nor was there any other form of acknowledgment. No one knew this, but the violinist was Joshua Bell, one of the most talented musicians in the world. He had just played one of the most intricate pieces ever written—on a violin worth $3.5 million dollars. Two days before his playing in the subway, Joshua Bell sold out at a theater in Boston, where the seats averaged $100. This is a real story. As part of a social experiment, the *Washington Post* had organized Bell's playing incognito in the Metro station.

> Whatever your circumstance,
> be confident that what
> you can't see readily
> might still be there.

How many other things have you missed because of your failure to recognize an opportunity since the outward circumstances didn't necessitate your attention? When you draw abrupt conclusions about any condition, chances are you will never see the boundless possibilities available. Sometimes the only requirement to experience amazing things in your life is a belief that anything is possible. What we see as a blessing or a curse may simply be part of the preparation for what lies ahead. Be careful interpreting change as disaster. I have spent a lifetime witnessing people go through expected and unwelcome change, and have enjoyed seeing many move on to opportunity, freedom, fulfillment and wealth. Whatever your circumstance, be confident that what you can't see readily might still be there. Be slow to jump to conclusions. Only God knows the final story.

Red Rover and Fireflies

Five decades ago, there was no need for the National Football League to produce "Play 60" commercials that encouraged children to go outside and play for 60 minutes a day. Before there was Internet and all the technology of the modern era, children actually played from the moment they woke up until the moment their parents yelled for them to come back inside for homework or bedtime. In the summertime, it was particularly common for kids to spend all day outside, breaking only for lunch and dinner, the meals my mother required us to sit down for. Even more rare was the fact that we would eat our meals at the kitchen table with the entire family.

> In order to make permanent changes, you have to be willing.

Fifty years later, the world has changed considerably, and baby boomers disagree about why children don't spend as much time outside as they did themselves. Studies show, sadly enough, that children now spend less than 30 minutes a week playing outdoors. Once a child has a cell phone, use of that phone will become one of the more nuanced and complicated issues that you deal with. However, a study of 1,000 parents revealed that 80 percent admitted they have never taken their children stargazing or fishing, and 90 percent confessed to not even going outside with their children. According to parents, homework, computer games and weather are the three biggest reasons their children spend less time doing outdoor activities. The reality is that when baby boomers were growing up there wasn't 24-hour children's programming on television. We didn't have to be concerned about safety in the same ways we do today, either. Additionally, many parents over-schedule and over-extend their children, denying them opportunities to have the same kind of simple fun they were fortunate enough to have themselves.

Kids need unstructured playtime so they can take a break from thinking. Whatever happened to hide-and-seek, red rover, catching fireflies, red light green light, tag, jump rope, ring around the rosie, freeze tag, four squares, kickball and other games you and your friends just made up on the fly? Several factors have contributed to the demise of outside play over the years. More mothers working, more TV channels available, the popularity of handheld video games, the invention of Internet and modern-day safety concerns. But maybe the question you need to ask yourself is, "When is the last time you, as a parent, went outside and taught your children how to play these games?" Receptiveness is about willingness. Are you willing to see things differently? To change? To experience new ideas? When you encounter a detour, how you advance from there won't be based on your ability. Your triumph will be based on your willingness.

A Culture of Opportunity

The 4,154th Marriott Hotel opened in the Caribbean. On the surface, it seemed like a standard-issue Marriott—a modern concrete structure with a giant "M" on top, 175 rooms, ample meeting space, a nice pool outside with palm trees and orange umbrellas, all nestled in the hills with the island's mountains rising in the distance.

But this is not just any Marriott; it's the Marriott Port-au-Prince Hotel, in the hard, hot country of Haiti, and its very existence is a testimony to Marriott's unusually strong commitment to its people.

Marriott employs many Haitian Americans at its South Florida location. Bill Marriott, the company's executive chairman and its CEO for 40 years, until 2012, spends every January at the Fort Lauderdale Marriott Harbor Beach and has come to know these employees personally.

So, when the earthquake that devastated the country hit in 2010, he wanted to do something to help. The company and Marriott personally provided disaster relief, but Kathleen Matthews, the company's EVP and chief global communications and public affairs officer, pitched a bigger idea. Why not build a hotel in Haiti instead, which would continue to give back in the form of jobs, economic activity and opportunity for local suppliers? While this is not a conventional hotel market, it's a testament to the Marriott culture of opportunity.

The result was a unique partnership with Digicel Group and the Clinton Foundation. So, while at first glance the hotel is pure

Marriott, inside are local touches like papier-mâché skulls hanging on the wall behind the check-in desk and traditional Haitian tin art. Coffee is sourced from a local grower; produce comes from a farmer's co-op in the nearby mountains; the fair-trade soaps in the room are supplied by a small business that employs Haitian women. On hand for the hotel's soft opening were Bill Clinton, Sean Penn, Haiti president Michel Martelly, Digicel Group chairman Denis O'Brien and other dignitaries—as well as many of the hotel's 130 full-time staffers, who were beaming.

Marriott—a company who exemplifies the mindset of receptiveness and the belief of possibilities.

*Use your smile
to change the world,
but don't let the world
change your smile.*

THE MINDSET OF
RESOLUTION

Unearthing the Power of Determination

res·o·lu·tion

ˌre-zə-ˈlü-shən

noun

1. the state or quality of being resolute; firm determination.

2. a resolving to do something.

3. a course of action determined or decided on.

Staying the Course

How do you know when it's the right time to make a change and begin to take the small steps that will hopefully lead you to success and a more positive life? Perhaps a more appropriate question is how will you feel if you don't make a change at all? Picture yourself then. Change doesn't need to be a colossal plunge. It might simply be a shift in attitude or a new approach to something. If it feels too daunting, you can probably break it down into smaller, less risky steps. Feeling at least a little anxious when you face a detour is normal, but don't let fear prevent you from heading in the right direction. The instant you decide to be positive, you will point yourself toward your accomplishment.

> When barriers appear, it's normal to change direction, but don't lessen your resolve to get there.

On the other hand, if you think, "This is never going to work out," every facet of your being will deflate and give up the fight. Sure, there will be days and weeks when you'll want to stay in bed and pull the covers over your head. Resilience can be learned, however. Be strong. People with the mindset of resolution focus on what they have rather than on what they don't have. They accept their present circumstance and make the most of it. They are grateful for what they have and are realistically optimistic.

When life frustrates you, fuel yourself with resolve. At the end of the day, life is hard for all of us. You might look at successful people from the outside and think they have it. You might think you're putting in as much effort as someone else. The truth is, we often overestimate our own determination and underestimate the determination of those around us.

A Lesson from Nike

As 2014 ended, I contemplated what differences I wanted to make in the future and which parts of my life are fine just as they are. I listed my priorities, including practical considerations, and recognized that I needed to make some drastic changes and restore balance where some boundaries have been overstepped. My challenge—just doing it!

In 1988, Nike launched their "Just Do It" campaign. Not only did it brand their company in an astonishing way, it inspired people to push themselves towards success, to simply get off their butts and accomplish things. Easier said than done! The phrase "Just Do It" doesn't offer much wiggle room. Then again, that's the point.

> Openness and honesty are the sunlight necessary to make effective and efficient decisions.

Most people will find themselves at a career crossroads at some point in their lives. For me, it wasn't so much a crossroads as it was a desire to simplify a multifaceted existence. Knowing it would be difficult to do this objectively, I sought the counsel of friends, family and professional colleagues. I am a firm believer that openness and honesty are the sunlight necessary to make effective and efficient decisions. I discussed all of my options to make sure my decisions were thoroughly explored rather than arrived at emotionally.

With everyone's help, I made some robust choices that have, candidly, surprised a lot of people. From selling my Pittsburgh Steelers seat licenses at Heinz Field, which I have owned for three decades, to selling shares in a company I co-founded, I was determined to make sweeping changes. I even scrutinized my philanthropic undertakings. While I have found my altruistic endeavors rewarding, I also felt overwhelmed at times by these various activities. Based on the counsel of my primary supporters, I withdrew my involvement with certain benevolent events. This decision was based exclusively on my objective to restore balance in my life. Four sons, four grandsons and aging parents can produce a variety of detours that can profoundly readdress your priorities. I am well aware that all good things must come to an end and, thus far, I have had an incredible ride. I just want to make sure I end it on the right note and don't look back with any doubts.

A Lesson from a Friend

A good friend of mine, who is an amazing speaker, author and person, is also a supporter of mine. While I have never ceremoniously defined Scott Burrows as a mentor, he truly is a person who has guided and motivated me through his own resolution. People define success in many ways. To him, it's simple: Success is who we are, what we believe in and what we ourselves think it means to be successful. For some, that means money; for others, relationships, family, jobs, religion or education. To Scott, success is deciding what you want, then acting on it. It is reaching your personal dreams while contributing to the lives of others—and being able to accomplish things independently. Scott has achieved his goals on his own terms and at his own pace.

> Perseverance, willpower and goal setting are infectious.

Scott played college football at Florida State University under legendary coach Bobby Bowden as a walk-on wide receiver and was a top-ranked kick boxing champion, having his last fight broadcast by ESPN. Later that year, his life took a dramatic turn when he was involved in a serious accident that left him paralyzed from the chest down and diagnosed a quadriplegic. Despite this grim prognosis, Scott refused to be sidelined. After graduating from college, he became a top producer in the financial and insurance industry, qualifying for the Million Dollar Round Table—a 100% commission-driven sales award—before forming Global Golf Group, a successful, international, family-run firm specializing in golf course development. Scott employs his paralysis as a visual metaphor. He encourages his audiences to stand up to their challenges—regardless of circumstances—and achieve their absolute best by developing the mindset of resolution. His perseverance, willpower and goal setting are infectious. Scott is a shining example of how success is determined by how well you adapt to change, doubt, uncertainty and fear.

You Can If You Will

Our brains have absolutely unbelievable power! One thing they do is very effectively filter and sort information. This is a huge benefit to us, but can also cause a lot of problems. When you start thinking about what you want, your brain auto-filters out possibilities before you even really consider them. Your brain tells you, "That's not realistic, so don't entertain it" or "That seems unreasonable; you can't do that." One of the most influential words you will ever use or hear is can't. We often equate *can't* with *impossible*. On the contrary! All it means is that the person saying it has reached the limits of what they think is possible. When someone says, "I can't do it," what they are actually saying is "I don't want to do this because I've always done it a certain way." With the right mindset, positive attitude and a clear vision of what you want to accomplish, the only things holding you back are yourself and the no-changes policy you have established. By saying you can't do something, you already doubt yourself, submitting to defeat and making that barrier around your life tighter.

> Before you say you can't
> do something, take
> one step toward it.

Change is unlearning habits and breaking conditioned responses. You do things a certain way, chances are you've been doing them for years. To stop yourself from saying the forbidden word, treat it as the worst profanity you could possibly utter. Cut yourself off mid-sentence if you must and turn your whole perspective around. Repetition, repetition, repetition! Change will not occur overnight. When I catch myself saying I can't do something or I don't know something, educating myself on the subject relieves my uncertainty. Sometimes a task seems too daunting. Before you say you can't do something, take one step toward it. Then another. Before you know it, you will have accomplished a previously "impossible" goal. Once you establish this habit and really start noticing some change, you'll realize the door to opportunity is everywhere. You write a book one morning, one sentence and one day at a time. You *can* write a book, play the piano, go back to school, cook or change jobs. Remember, nothing is impossible when you put your amazing mind to it.

Wait for It...Wait for It

Writer and humorist Arnold Glasgow said, "The key to everything is patience. You get the chicken by hatching the egg, not by smashing it open." Impatience not only hurts us, but the people around us. It can raise our stress levels, damage relationships and obstruct our path to realizing our ambitions. Life moves at a frenetic, fast-forward, Instagram pace. The ability to tolerate any delay has become ever more challenging. Patience creates feelings of peace and calm, as opposed to anger and frustration.

Your resolve in any situation is based on your ability to muster patience even when it goes against every fiber of your being while waiting in a doctor's office, sitting in a traffic jam or waiting for your children to do something you asked them to do an hour ago.

> The people who succeed in life are those who are willing to do what they don't feel like doing.

I have come to understand that patience is made up of various aspects, with persistence being one of them. Having the capacity to keep going even when you can't see the end result is how you make your dreams come true. The more important your goal is, the longer it's going to take to achieve and the more discipline it's going to require. Nothing great is ever accomplished without persistence and patience because, in order to be successful, your dreams must translate into work. The people who succeed in life are those who are willing to do what they don't feel like doing. Sometimes you have to delay gratification. Do the tough thing instead of the fun thing, the right thing instead of the pleasurable thing. Impatience is how we accumulate debt. We say, "I want it now, and since I can't afford it I'll put it on a credit card." Any goal you deem worthwhile is going to be guarded by obstacles. Focus on the long-term so that, when a detour comes, you can persevere confident that you are going to get past it and be that much closer to your objective.

Must Be Nice

I have hosted several speakers and authors at my home over the past fifteen years, and occasionally someone has remarked, "Must be nice!" I don't believe they mean it in a cruel way towards me, but more as a judgment on themselves. They perceive my success as something they desire but aren't sure they can realize for themselves. When I hear the word *success*, I immediately think of *patience* and *persistence*, too. Having experienced many failures and successes in my life, I've learned that nothing can be achieved without those two words. *Patience* means being ready to face detours, to accept accidents and, in many cases, to undergo trials in the pursuit of a desired objective. *Persistence* means not giving up—keeping focused to the bitter end.

> Not until you see failure as a lack of persistence and patience will you ever arrive at your desired end.

Certainly, many of us lack patience and persistence. Speakers want what I have, but they want it the easy way. When I see someone unwilling to sacrifice time, effort or whatever is necessary, I am not surprised when they fail. Oddly enough, they rarely seem to hold themselves accountable for their own failures. When they start blaming people or circumstances, it's almost impossible to guide them in the right direction. Not until you see failure as a lack of persistence and patience will you ever arrive at your desired end. Those who persist no matter what the obstacles, who are prepared to battle the winds no matter what the cost, will sooner or later succeed. Whatever obstacles you face, it's *your* responsibility to turn them into growth opportunities and transform negativity into positivity. Behind my office building is a large dumpster that contains our marketing and product flops. I've always believed that every time we fail we eliminate a wrong way to do something, making our path toward success that much more navigable. Those who truly fail are those who give up trying.

Your Harvest Will Come

"As someone who's witnessed you transform from the ambitious but penniless guy you were 17 years ago into a man with so many blessings in his life, I'm just so happy for you and proud to call you my friend. You continue to make a huge difference in my life, and that's something I will never forget." That statement was made by a friend you will come to know better later in the book. Mike Murray said this referencing the day he handed me a $5.00 bill to purchase a bagel and coffee at a Bruegger's in Monroeville, Pennsylvania. It was February 17, 1999. Mike was one of the few people back then who saw my vision and believed in it. Unlike everyone else who only saw me watering a whole lot of dirt, Mike envisioned my harvest.

> Never allow anyone who can't see your vision to dissuade you or influence you to abandon or neglect it.

For the past several years, Mike has witnessed the seeds I've been planting with blood, sweat, tears and lack of sleep. I never allowed anyone who couldn't see my vision to dissuade me or influence me to abandon or neglect it. Mike Murray could always see the roots and what was budding under the dirt. That isn't to suggest there weren't any weeds and that a few things didn't die along the way, but I never lost my faith in the fact that the harvest would come. Maybe the most important factor was I never lost sight of why I planted the seeds in the first place. I was determined to impact people and make a difference in their lives.

Who's Counting?

James Dyson built 5,126 failed prototypes of his vacuum cleaner. How many times are you willing to try something with no end in sight?

- Steven Spielberg was rejected by the University of Southern California Film School 3 times

- Tim Ferris's book *The 4-Hour Work Week* was rejected by publishers 25 times

- The founder of Pandora.com approached investors 300 times before he got funding

- Richard Branson launched companies 400 times before he finally founded Virgin Atlantic

- Colonel Sanders, founder of KFC, was turned down 1,009 times when he tried selling his fried chicken recipe

o Sylvester Stallone was rejected 1,500 times when he tried selling his script and himself for what would become the iconic film *Rocky*.

So how do you do it? How do you stay persistent and not give up? First and foremost, remind yourself that most successes are not overnight. Only 1% of startups ever produce more than $1 million in revenue, and less than 1% are overnight wonders. Secondly, try new things in new ways. When 99 things fail, reach down and find the resolve to try number 100. A person who makes no mistakes is unlikely to make anything at all. It's better to have 99 small failures that you learn from than a lifetime filled with the regret of never having tried. If you don't like something, change it. If you can't change it, change the way you think about it. Winston Churchill reminds us, "Success is moving from one failure to another with no loss of enthusiasm." Your mind must believe before it can be capable. Lastly, and most importantly, accept that mistakes will happen. Life didn't come with an instruction book. Your mistakes and failures should be your motivation, not your excuse. Never be afraid to make a mistake. They teach you important lessons. No matter how chaotic the past has been, the future is a wide-open slate.

The Success of Others Isn't Personal

Let's just say that being happy for others didn't come naturally to me. I grew up in a family where I competed with my brother and cousins. If you told a story at a family gathering, somebody would chime in about how they did what you did better. You begin to get jealous and find yourself focusing solely on yourself and your happiness. While on the subject, remember that jealous people raise jealous kids. Being happy for others isn't easy when you have a competitive spirit. Have you ever found yourself in a funk about something and you weren't sure why? Maybe your coworker got a promotion, your sister got her master's degree or your friend just moved into a lavish house in the suburbs. When you're able to feel happiness simply because others are happy, you gain a fresh perspective in life.

> When you admit that you're jealous and let go of it, you will feel unburdened.

Growing up, I would watch other children open presents at their birthday parties and be envious. I would see the new bicycles, gloves and toys, realizing my mom couldn't afford them. Though I was never angry with her, I was unable to feel good for the kids who had things I didn't. Worse yet, I was unable to be happy just by seeing them happy. In high school, I didn't like the quarterback on our football team, although I didn't know him at all. I thought he was perky and way too popular. It wasn't until later in life—after I'd made a conscious effort to be more upbeat and develop more friendships—that I realized I'd written off a lot of people without even knowing them. As you get older, the stakes are different. You might envy the big house, the new car or someone's career. Ask yourself, "Would it kill me to be happy for this person? If I just let go of my envy, what would that cost me?" When you admit that you're jealous and let go of it, you will feel unburdened. The success of others isn't personal. They aren't out to spite you. In fact, what someone else does or owns has nothing to do with you. Eliminate your own desires from the equation so you can feel relief or happiness for another person. That kind of an attitude will help you to move forward.

No U-Turns

Chances are, when you arrive at a detour in life, you'll be tired. Your problems will have multiplied and, even worse, they'll seem to be ganging up on you. Instead of focusing on the roadblock and any anxiety it might be causing you, focus on how far you have already come. Resolve to face your problems—because they are not going away. Most of my problems weren't anywhere near as bad as I thought once I took some time to really study them. Our imagination can run wild and is all too often our biggest enemy. We have the unfortunate ability to turn nothing into something and small issues into major ordeals—then we run away. The way our world works is that running in the opposite direction of trouble or complication eventually leads you right back to your point of origin. We can save ourselves so much time and energy by facing things head on or, better yet, not making such a big deal out of them in the first place.

> Not until I faced my own issues did I begin to overcome them.

I used to believe that relationship problems would get better if I simply ignored them. It never happened that way, of course. But then, I also used to hope I would win the lottery without buying a ticket. We run away because of what we fear might happen, not because of the reality of the situation. Yet, we allow our imagination to make poor decisions. I will always remember the morning my second wife announced she was leaving me after 22 months of marriage. Not only was I devastated, I was also afraid of what my family, friends and colleagues would think about me. Even after the divorce was settled, I would never bring it up. How could I? I was a successful author and speaker who traveled the world spreading a message of optimism, courage and hope. Not until I faced my own demons did I begin to overcome them. My starting point was a simple decision. I woke up one morning and realized that, while nothing in my life might stay the same, one thing that should remain unbroken is my heart.

My mother always taught me to be strong, good, kind, humble, true and honest. Make these qualities permanent fixtures in your own heart. When your heart feels like giving up, give it a rest, but never give up. Don't allow a detour to stop you or cause you to turn around. Hold your head high. Stop letting your imagination be your guide, and stop praying when it rains if you don't pray when the sun shines. Think about a few things you're afraid of or uncomfortable with—some difficulties or problems in your life. Pick one and take that first action step toward facing and overcoming it. It starts with a decision. Make it and you're halfway there. Turning around at a detour will never get you where you want to end up. Keep your eyes forward and appreciate that every challenge makes you stronger and gets you that much closer to your destination.

Game-Changers—
The Mindset of Resolution

The ability to withstand failure is a quality inherent not only to inventors but also to scientists, artists, celebrities, entrepreneurs and public figures.

Here are some game-changers who faced failure or rejection before finally succeeding.

J.K Rowling

The author of the *Harry Potter* series didn't magically become wealthier than the Queen of England. Impoverished and divorced, she wrote the first book on an old typewriter, only to encounter rejection by more than ten publishers. A year later, a publisher named Barry Cunningham accepted her book, but suggested she get another job because children's books typically produced meager profits.

David Sanders

Better known as Colonel Sanders and the founder of KFC, this entrepreneur was already 65 when he started his franchise. In his early years, he worked many odd and low-paying jobs, from farmhand to streetcar conductor and steamboat operator. After creating a secret chicken recipe, Sanders started a small restaurant. But, in 1955, his restaurant failed after a new highway cut off customer access.

Instead of giving up, Sanders drove around America trying to sell his restaurant concept, only to hear "no" countless times before he raked in millions from a Kentucky businessman who was willing to buy his recipe.

Steve Jobs

Even if you now consider your iPhone, Mac or iPad indispensable, a decade ago you might have dismissed Apple products altogether. Jobs' Apple III computer, the early model of the Mac, was so poorly designed that the computer earned a reputation as an unreliable machine that invariably crashed because of poor ventilation. After Jobs was fired from Apple, the company he co-founded, he designed the NeXT hardware, which sold poorly at first but later became the foundation for future Apple products. And the rest is history.

In order to claim fame, these people and others were faced with obstacles that required them to embrace their mistakes and show great determination. Whatever your goal, remember that failure—often, many failures—precede success. If you treat each failure as an opportunity to learn and to dig down even deeper inside yourself to find that resolve, you'll be that much more likely to succeed.

A CANDID CONVERSATION

Hall of Fame Speaker and best-selling Author Steve Gilliland sat down with Advantage Media Group's CEO, Adam Witty, for a candid conversation. In this Q&A, Adam pulls back the curtain and inquires about Steve...

...the speaker...

...the businessman...

...the author...

...and the person.

Q: **If a genie promised you a *New York Times* #1 best-selling book that sold over 100 million copies in exchange for never being able to speak again, would you accept that offer?**

A: My passion is speaking, hence, I would never trade the joy of speaking for all the money and notoriety a book like that would produce. Then again, ask me that question when I am 80 years old, not 56.

Q: **If you had a time machine and could travel to any year and hear any speaker and speech, where would you go?**

A: August 28, 1963. Washington, DC. Martin Luther King. I would love to have been there to hear his "*I Have A Dream*" speech, which was the greatest demonstration for freedom in the history of our nation. When I think about all of the people who made a difference in this world, he is definitely in my top 5.

Q: **Do you ever get mistaken for a celebrity?**

A: If I had a nickel for every time someone said, "You remind me a lot of Jay Leno," I would have several dollars. While I understand the comparison, I am also sometimes surprised. I guess my salt-and-pepper hair and mannerisms are slightly similar. The thing is, Jay Leno doesn't have a goatee, and I am confident my chin is somewhat smaller.

Q: **Where is a place you've never been to that you would like to visit?**

A: Egypt. An item on my bucket list is to visit the Seven Wonders of the World. The Great Pyramid of Giza, also known as the Pyramid of Khufu or Pyramid of Cheops, which is the oldest of the Seven Wonders of the Ancient World and the only one to remain largely intact.

Q: **Where did your first paycheck come from?**

A: Dairy Queen. When I was 16, my first job was working there, and it was great. I worked the grill and counter and met a lot of nice people. Of course, "all the ice cream you can consume for free" was a huge benefit. Later in life you get a lot of great remunerations from employers, but endless ice cream is tough to beat.

Q: **You sign your name undoubtedly hundreds of times every week, but whose autograph did you get as a kid that seemed to be a big deal to you at the time?**

A: Roberto Clemente, and it is still a big deal as an adult. As a child growing up in the Pittsburgh area, I had the benefit of attending games at the legendary Forbes Field. We always tried to sit in the right field stands, which were in close proximity to the playing field. In addition to playing 18 seasons for the

Pittsburgh Pirates and being a National League MVP, four-time batting champion and twelve-time Gold Glove winner, Clemente was involved in charity work in Puerto Rico, Latin America and Caribbean countries during the off seasons. He died in an aviation accident on December 31, 1972 en route to deliver aid to earthquake victims in Nicaragua.

Q: **Most people are addicted to their phone; however, those who know you find your indifference towards operating a mobile device interesting. How have you avoided getting caught up in the up-to-the-minute technological paraphernalia?**

A: I might get in trouble for saying this, but I steadfastly believe it is a matter of choice, and most people choose to overindulge in their usage. Priorities dictate your choices, and your choices determine your daily path. I choose not to talk, post, tweet or text like the average person because I have other priorities that supersede the phone. I am not against talking, texting or social media. I just sense that, like so many other things, people lack the discipline to use it in moderation. Like any addiction, continued use of your phone becomes compulsive and eventually interferes with ordinary life responsibilities.

$Q:$ **When a person who has heard you speak criticizes you, what is your preferred method of dealing with them?**

$A:$ First and foremost, what may shock some people is that I personally respond to all criticism. Thankfully, I haven't had too many people who didn't enjoy me speaking. When I am evaluated negatively, I always try to learn something from the criticism. I prefer to talk directly to them as opposed to responding via the Internet.

$Q:$ **Are you willing to share an incident where someone criticized you and it was hard for you to accept and respond back to them positively?**

$A:$ Absolutely! Lubbock, Texas. There was a Baptist minister who attended a community event I was hired to speak at. When I introduced my mom, as I always do, I paid tribute to her by proclaiming that she is a King James Version, front row, Bible-carrying fundamental Baptist. Additionally, I told a lighthearted story about her and, as ALWAYS, I asserted how thankful I am to have been raised at the knee of a highly Christian-principled woman. When the event was over, I received a scathing email from this minister, who criticized me for "making fun" of my mother and her religious beliefs. The letter was so contemptuous that I shared it with my mom. Without my encouragement, she sent a seven-page, handwritten letter in response. Here is an excerpt: *Make sure that you are willing to be judged by the same standard of judgment. In my 60-plus years of being a Christian, I have always warned my son about self-deception and hypocrisy. How well do you know my son? How about before you judge him you get to know him? I have always told my son, people will hurt you, as you have. However, God will heal you. People will try to humiliate you, as your email has. However, God will magnify you. People will judge you, as you have. However, God will justify you. You may not have the same kind of relationship with your parents that my son has with me; however, my son honors God and me every time he speaks. I would rather have him subtly weave God into his public and corporate presentations by exercising humor than have him do like so many other Christian speakers and not even acknowledge their faith for fear of criticism. Gandhi once stated that he would have been a Christian if it were not for Christians. Hmmmm.* The beautiful part about his critical email, and my mother's subsequent response, was that we never heard from him again. Surprise!

Q: **If you could interview any person in the world who is still living, who would it be, and what would be the most candid question you would ask?**

A: William Franklin "Billy" Graham. In the past 96 years, what would you deem the greatest DETOUR you ever faced?

Q: **When you think about all of the books you have written and speeches you have presented, what do you believe is the most valued piece of information you shared with people?**

A: Cure your destination disease. I just believe that if people could learn to live more for today, less for tomorrow and never about yesterday, they would live longer, healthier and happier lives. Each of us tends to live beyond the moment and we miss so much.

Here are a few more "rapid-fire" questions...

Q: What was the last lie you told?

A: Moments ago, I told you how much I enjoyed these interview questions.

Q: Best compliment you have received?

A: I was recently approached at a book signing after I finished speaking, and a woman thanked me for being so unpretentious.

Q: Strangest compliment you ever received?

A: You look thinner from the back of the room.

Q: What is your perfect pizza?

A: Classic Margherita Pizza New York Style that I am eating while in New York City.

Q: What is your favorite adult beverage?

A: Scotch.

Q: What's the one show or movie you're embarrassed to admit you watch?

A: *Rudolph the Red-Nosed Reindeer.* I have watched it every year since it first aired in December 1964.

Q: What was your first car?

A: 1967 Plymouth Valiant.

Q: What is your biggest pet peeve?

A: Families on their mobile devices at dinner in a restaurant.

Q: What was the first concert you attended?

A: Three Dog Night.

Q: What is your favorite late night snack?

A: Ice cream.

Q: If you could have personally witnessed anything, what would you want to have seen?

A: I would have wanted to be in the front row to see Elvis Presley's concert "Aloha from Hawaii" on January 14, 1973. It took place at the Honolulu International

Center in Honolulu (now known as the Neal S. Blaisdell Center) and aired in over 40 countries across Asia and Europe (who received the telecast the next day, also in primetime). Ironically, the United States didn't air the concert until April 4, 1973 because it took place the same day as Super Bowl VII.

Q: Would you be willing to lie to a court for your best friend if it meant saving your friend from going to jail for life?

A: No.

Q: What is your favorite word and least favorite word?

A: My favorite word is hope. My least favorite word is impossible.

Q: What is your favorite "corny" joke?

A: Horse walks into a bar and the bartender says, "What's with the long face?"

Q: Is the glass half empty or half full?

A: Depends on if you're pouring or drinking.

Q: What is the strangest thing you have ever eaten?

A: Rocky Mountain Oysters. Main ingredients: testicles (bull calf, sometimes pig or sheep), flour, pepper and salt.

Q: If you could bring any person back to life, who would it be?

A: My grandma Stevenson (Carrie). She was awesome! When I was growing up, I loved staying at her house. She made homemade bread, soup and donuts. She was a good woman who loved her family and was loved by all. It wasn't the holidays until we went to Grandma's house.

Q: If you had to be trapped in a television show for a month, which would you choose?

A: *America's Got Talent.* I love to laugh and be entertained. The time would pass faster, and I am sure I would meet a lot of unique, gifted and good people.

Q: List someone you know and describe them in five words.

A: My wife, Diane. Resilient, caring, patient, loving and hot!

Q: When was the last time you went for a jog?

A: Yesterday. It was raining in Lafayette, Louisiana, and I jogged from the hotel parking lot to the lobby. Does that count?

Q: What do you think Victoria's Secret is?

A: She loves flannel.

Q: What is your favorite breakfast food?

A: Eggs Benedict.

Q: What is the last thing your wife cooked that you didn't like?

A: My goose!

Q: If you could have one meal for the rest of your life, what would it be?

A: My wife's spaghetti.

Q: What was your favorite venue to speak at?

A: Mel Brooks' Theater in Las Vegas at the Paris Hotel.

Q: What was the last picture you took on your phone?

A: You're kidding, right? I have eight pictures in my iPhoto library, and someone else took all eight. I said earlier that I am not a big phone guy, so the notion of taking pictures is not something that electrifies me.

Q: You and your wife, Diane, have a blended family with each of you bringing two boys into the marriage. If you would have had a child with her, what gender would you have wanted and what would you have named him or her?

A. Isn't that pretty obvious? I would have wanted a girl. I would have hoped to name her Diana. I would have wanted my daughter to live her life knowing she was named after a princess—her mom!

WITHOUT THE FOLLOWING, I COULD NEVER HAVE WRITTEN THIS BOOK.

THANK YOU FOR THE GIFT OF...

Relaxation

Bella Mia Spa & Skin Care Center (Advance, NC)

Susan Locke, the owner of Bella Mia, handpicks her staff. Members include fully licensed estheticians, massage therapists and nail technicians. While the staff is fully accredited and exceptionally talented, that is not what separates them from their competition. From the moment you are welcomed at the front desk, the complete staff initiate an experience that you will never forget. I received numerous massages while writing *DETOUR*. A special thank you to Susan for handpicking **Linda Robinson**, an extraordinary massage therapist and a remarkable person. Linda's passion, professionalism and nurturing personality is second to none. The moment I met her she was interested in my health, family and well-being. As I wrote the pages of this book, she presented valuable insight on the various topics we discussed. In addition to a wonderful massage therapist, she always takes time to share and care. Although the book is complete, I will forever be a patron. Thank you, Bella Mia, for the gift of relaxation.

Loyalty

Pearhouse Productions (Pittsburgh, PA)

Mike Murray, the owner of Pearhouse Productions, is an accomplished editor and writer. His plays have been produced for the stage, his short stories have been published in literary journals throughout the land, and during his days in Hollywood he worked in public relations for TV shows such as *Dynasty, The Love Boat* and *It's a Living*. When he traded coasts, he joined the editorial staffs of *Longevity* and *Condé Nast Traveler*, both New York-based magazines. Then one day he decided to move to Pittsburgh and start his own company. Mike is a brilliant graphic designer who specializes in print and web development, but that is only one of his talents. His extraordinary gifts also include humility and loyalty. Seventeen years after he designed my corporate logo and business card, he is the principal editor of everything I write, and our corporation has become his largest client. While his last name is not Gilliland, and he is not on our payroll, he is loved by all and recognized as part of our family. Thanks, Mike, for your gift of loyalty.

Perspective

Slo-Motion Speed Shop (Mocksville, NC)

As I have said previously, it is easier to write a best-selling book than to live one. When I wrote *Enjoy The Ride*, there was more than one person who hurled it back at me by expressing, "Hey Steve, don't forget to enjoy the ride!" **Chris Porter**, who owns Slo-Motion Speed Shop and works full-time at Detroit Speed in Mooresville, North Carolina, has been preaching this to me since we first met in the summer of 2008. After considerable cajoling, Chris convinced me to purchase a 1981 Corvette. He also stressed that I needed to drive it, not look at it. Not only have I driven it, but on any given summer Saturday morning I am home, it isn't uncommon for Diane and me to take the top off the car and just start driving. When someone asks where we are heading, I always respond, "Not sure, but I will certainly know when I arrive." Whether it's a 73-mile drive on a state road to eat breakfast at an out-of-the way diner or a 47-mile drive to Mount Airy, North Carolina to visit Floyd's City Barbershop, Chris had the right idea. Take a drive with no destination in mind, no agenda and just clear your mind for a day. He has the right outlook. Drive a really fast car slowly and enjoy the ride! Thanks, Chris, for the gift of perspective.

Laughter

The Laugh Factory Comedy
Network (Los Angeles, CA)

Steve Rizzo has appeared as a national headline comedian with opening acts such as Drew Carey, Rosie O'Donnell and Dennis Miller. Additionally, Steve has the distinction of hosting his own SHOWTIME special. He is one of the funniest people I know. His paramount strength is comedy; however, what makes him special is his genuine desire to help people. His purpose and passion is teaching people how to be happy and successful no matter what the circumstance, and I am honored to call him my friend. Steve has always answered my calls, never once turned down a single request and instantly makes me laugh regardless of my state of mind. In the midst of writing the final chapter for this book, I extended an invitation for him to join me in Charleston, South Carolina. I wanted to share an idea with him and get his opinion on a project related to the book. Not only did he fly down and connect with me on the book endeavor, he joined me on stage at the event where I was speaking. He made us all laugh hysterically and then stuck around to talk with people afterward. He has constantly had the ability to make me laugh when I needed it most and be there for me when I needed it more. Thank you, Steve, for the gift of laughter.

Serenity

Home (Mocksville, NC)

In June of 2008, we relocated from a house to a home and a perfect setting in which to write. We live in an area that provides an abundance to enjoy, which elegantly blends the outdoors and indoor living spaces. Covered porches, rocking chairs, multiple decks, heated pool and a fire pit complete with Adirondack chairs are just a few of the features that make up our sanctuary of tranquility. Overlooking 26 acres, it is common to wake up and enjoy a fresh cup of coffee on the screened porch watching the deer feed in a section of woods that has been specifically cleared for this purpose. Our home embodies peacefulness and captures the essence of what it means to embrace the great outdoors—complete with a Go-Kart track for all of the children and grandchildren to enjoy. Grandpa, too. It is a refuge for me after traveling and speaking. When someone asks me my favorite vacation spot, I don't hesitate to say, "My home!" Maya Angelou once said, "The ache for home lives in all of us. The safe place where we can go as we are and not be questioned." Thank you, God, for all your blessings and for the gift of my home.

Laugh when you can,

apologize when you should,

and let go of what you can't change.

Life's too short to be
anything...but happy.

FINAL THOUGHT

Someone once said, "A truly happy person is one who can enjoy the scenery on a detour. Although this book was not intended to be a sequel to *Enjoy The Ride*, if you really reflect on the content, *DETOUR* is an additive to what is necessary to enjoy the trip.

Have you ever been cruising through your day, only to be sidetracked by something unplanned? We all will face an unexpected problem to deal with, such as a sick child, a broken garage door as you are headed to work or an unhappy client, friend or supervisor. Some people will face even bigger detours, such as a job lost, unexpected death, car accident, unplanned pregnancy or a child addicted to drugs. Life is full of small and large unplanned detours. On the surface, it would be difficult to classify any of these as good. Our first response might be, "Why me?" "Why does this always happen to me?" "Why does this always happen to me when I'm so busy?"

As you move through life, always remember that you're not alone. As an author, I wanted to convey that I have come across many roads that were closed and have struggled to find a new path. It is frustrating! However, what I have found is that you must recognize, embrace and take the detour. It is the only way to keep moving forward. The detours you will face can turn out to be very positive and fulfilling. There's so much out there in our world, and sometimes it takes a detour to change our direction so we can experience everything life has to offer. You get a chance to meet new people, build new relationships and develop new ideas. The list is endless, especially if you are open to seeing the possibilities that exist. That is not to say that some detours won't be sad, frustrating or even tragic. However, even those roadblocks can provide an opportunity to learn and grow.

The next time you see "Road Closed Ahead," "Local Traffic Only" or "Detour," see it as an opportunity to experience new things. The moment it occurs, you may feel discouraged, upset and unhappy. Even if it doesn't feel like an opportunity just then, I am living proof that there is an abundance waiting for you if you allow it. Every detour will provide fresh scenery that you might have missed otherwise. Your life is full of amazing opportunities. Embrace the *Detour* and *Enjoy The Ride!*

THE STATION

By Robert J. Hastings

TUCKED AWAY in our subconscious minds is an idyllic vision in which we see ourselves on a long journey that spans an entire continent. We're traveling by train and, from the windows, we drink in the passing scenes of cars on nearby highways, of children waving at crossings, of cattle grazing in distant pastures, of smoke pouring from power plants, of row upon row upon row of cotton and corn and wheat, of flatlands and valleys, of city skylines and village halls.

But uppermost in our conscious minds is our final destination—for at a certain hour and on a given day, our train will finally pull into the Station with bells ringing, flags waving and bands playing. And once that day comes, so many wonderful dreams will come true. So restlessly, we pace the aisles and count the miles, peering ahead, waiting, waiting, waiting for the Station.

"Yes, when we reach the Station, that will be it!" we promise ourselves. "When we're eighteen...win that promotion...put the last kid through college...buy that 450SL Mercedes-Benz...have a nest egg for retirement!" From that day on we will all live happily ever after.

Sooner or later, however, we must realize there is no Station in this life, no one earthly place to arrive at once and for all. The journey is the joy. The Station is an illusion—it constantly out-distances us. Yesterday's a memory, tomorrow's a dream. Yesterday belongs to history, tomorrow belongs to God. Yesterday's a fading sunset, tomorrow's a faint sunrise. Only today is there light enough to love and live.

So, gently close the door on yesterday and throw the key away. It isn't the burdens of today that drive men mad, but rather the regret over yesterday and the fear of tomorrow. Regret and fear are twin thieves who would rob us of today.

"Relish the moment" is a good motto, especially when coupled with Psalm 118:24—"This is the day which the Lord hath made; we will rejoice and be glad in it."

So stop pacing the aisles and counting the miles. Instead, swim more rivers, climb more mountains, kiss more babies, count more stars. Laugh more and cry less. Go barefoot more often. Eat more ice cream. Ride more merry-go-rounds. Watch more sunsets. Life must be lived as we go along. The Station will come soon enough.

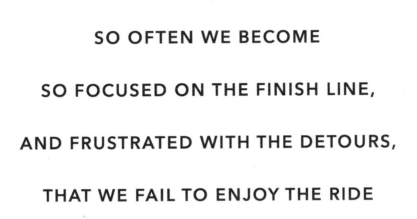

SO OFTEN WE BECOME

SO FOCUSED ON THE FINISH LINE,

AND FRUSTRATED WITH THE DETOURS,

THAT WE FAIL TO ENJOY THE RIDE

Steve Gilliland

April 13, 2015